T0266143

THE
CHAIN OF
TRADITION
SERIES

Volume I: Jewish Law

Illustrated by
Irwin Rosenhouse

THE
CHAIN OF
TRADITION
SERIES

Jewish Law

BY LOUIS JACOBS

Behrman House, Inc.

PUBLISHERS

for David

Copyright ©   1968 Louis Jacobs
Published by Behrman House, Inc.,
Springfield, NJ 07081
Library of Congress Catalog Card Number: 68-27329

Manufactured in the United States of America

International Standard Book Number: 0-87441-211-0

Introduction

JEWISH law is based on a central idea. Though ideals such as justice and mercy and holiness are very wonderful, to have any impact on human life they must be expressed in detailed action. For instance, the great Hebrew prophets preach to their people, and through them to us, that we should practice justice. Very well, we say, we are ready to heed the lesson. How do we go about it? For the answer to this it is not to the prophets that we can go but to those who followed them and strove mightily to put their ideas into operation. It is the Rabbis who answer in detail such questions as: what is a fair price? how can cheating be avoided? how should men conduct themselves in their daily business affairs? how should the Sabbath be made holy? how should a Synagogue be built? and so on through the whole range of Jewish experience.

Naturally not all the answers found in the older sources are appropriate to our day. In some of the texts presented here, for example, there are references to slaves because the laws in them came from an age when slavery had not yet been banished from human society. Even from these texts we can learn much. We can see, among other things, that the Jewish teachers tried to soften the rigors of slavery and taught that the slave should be treated as a human being. But, for all that, these texts have only academic interest nowadays since, thank God, in our world crude slavery is no more.

The picture which emerges from a study of Jewish law is one of ripe wisdom, the experience of generations of Jewish teachers, making itself felt in Jewish life. Not everything that was considered wise in former ages is so considered today. But what has come down to us in the sources represented by our texts is enough to inspire us to continue the creative task of translating Jewish ideals into concrete practices for the ennoblement of human life.

The material presented in this book is legal material, that is to say, it concerns itself with right and wrong, with what should be done and what should not be done. Questions of this kind are subtle. It is not easy to draw the fine lines which mark off the things to be done from the things to be rejected. Much argument is needed in order to arrive at a correct definition of the law and lawyers may frequently disagree on what the law is in a particular instance.

The really interesting aspects of a legal debate or discussion are to be found in the reasoning and argumentation rather than the final decision. You are advised therefore to be in no hurry to reach the end of any argument presented in these pages but to follow it through carefully, weighing up all the pros and cons. What makes a debate enjoyable is not the final vote. The fun of the debate consists in the skill and eloquence with which the contestants state their case.

This book, then, is to be read less like a novel than a text-book of mathematics. "Reading" is probably the wrong word here. The book should be "studied." Go over the various steps of each argument and ask yourself if you agree with them. It will be of help if the members of a class take sides and try to thrash the matter out for themselves. It should not be forgotten that practically all the cases mentioned in the book were debated by keen minds over many years. To obtain the best appreciation of the points raised a certain amount of reflection is demanded. "Go over it again and again" was the advice of the Rabbis of old to their pupils.

Furthermore, many of these discussions were originally verbal and were not written down until later. It is as if you are presented with the written reports of proceedings in a court of law. To obtain the best advantage of the material it will be necessary for you to reconstruct in your imagination the drama of the actual cases as they came before the courts.

This book contains selections from each of the main sources of Jewish law: (1) The Halakhic Midrashim; (2) The Mishnah; (3) The Jerusalem Talmud; (4) The Babylonian Talmud; (5) The Codes; (6) The Responsa. Each section is prefaced by a note describing its nature e.g. the section on the Mishnah is prefaced by a note describing what the Mishnah is, its date, authorship and so forth. In each section there are a number of items chosen to demonstrate the particular approach. The text is given in translation together with a point by point comment. Although the original texts have numbers indicating the divisions, these have not been utilized. The original text numbers can be easily determined by referring to the source listed at the beginning of each chapter.

When using the book you should first read the short note at the beginning of the section which contains the item you are studying. If, for example, you wish to read one of the items in the section on Codes, first read carefully the note which tells you what the Codes are. Then read the particular text, making sense of it with the aid of the commentary.

It will be found useful to have a Bible ready to hand and to look up in the Bible all the Biblical references in the text. The translation of Biblical texts has sometimes been changed slightly from that in the standard versions in order to make better sense of a particular Rabbinic comment. Sometimes the Rabbis had their own way of looking at a Biblical text.

Remember that most of these texts are hundreds of years old and have to be placed in a particular historical context, that is to say, they have to be seen against the background of their times. But most of the issues discussed take us to the heart of the Jewish ethical and legal approach and can, without too much difficulty, find their application in the kind of world in which we live.

The book can be studied systematically in the order in which the items are arranged, but if the reader so desires he can pick out any item which seems interesting to him and study it on its own. But the note to the section of which it is part should be read first of all. There is no need to worry about the identity of the various Rabbis and teachers mentioned in the text. These are fully discussed in the comment to the text. For further biographical information about the Rabbinic heroes it is a good idea to read the relevant articles in the Jewish Encyclopedia. There is an occasional overlapping of comment, i.e. some points have been made more than once in comments on different texts but this is to enable the reader to study any single text without having to read the whole book.

The aim should be, however, eventually to read through the whole book. If this is done it will be found that a fairly clear picture has been obtained of how Jewish law has grown through the ages and how it has operated in Jewish life.

The Halakhic Midrashim

THE HEBREW word *Halakhah* (hence the English form *Halakhic*) comes from the root *halakh* which means "to go." It represents the way in which a Jew should conduct himself, the rules and patterns of Jewish behavior and consequently it is a term for "Jewish law," for the legal side of Judaism. There is another Rabbinic term *Aggadah* (from a root meaning "to tell") and this represents all the stories, history, philosophy, folk-lore, science and the like found in Rabbinic literature. In short *Aggadah* embraces all the non-legal aspects of Judaism, *Halakhah* all the legal side of Judaism.

The word Midrash (plural Midrashim) comes from a root meaning "to inquire" or "to search" or "to examine." The basic idea is the examination of Scripture to make it yield more than lies on the surface. For instance, a close examination of the Scriptural references to the Sabbath will give us a clearer idea of what is meant by "work" on the Sabbath than a merely superficial reading would do. The great teachers of Judaism engaged for centuries in this kind of "search" or "inquiry" and their work has been collected in various forms. These works are known as the Midrashim.

Most of the Midrashim we now have are *Aggadic* in nature. But the earliest and those enjoying the greatest authority are *Halakhic*, hence the term *Halakhic Midrashim*. These date from the second century of the present era and earlier. The Rabbis of this period, whose views are found in the *Halakhic Midrashim*, are known as the *Tannaim* (plural of *Tanna*, "a teacher"). This word *Tannaim* is an Aramaic one, Aramaic being a sister language of Hebrew (like Dutch and German) and widely spoken in this and the next period. Hence another name for the *Halakhic Midrashim* is the *Tannaitic Midrashim*.

The period of the *Tannaim* is the first two centuries of the present era but the Midrashic process itself is much earlier going back to the time of Ezra, the fifth century B.C.E. Indeed, some of the material in these *Tannaitic Midrashim* is much earlier than the period of the *Tannaim*.

As will be seen from the examples given in this section, the *Halakhic Midrashim* are in the form of a running commentary to the legal portions of the Five Books of Moses. Verse by verse the passages are examined and the opinions of the Rabbis, often differing opinions, are quoted. The whole process has the aim of connecting the law to the Scriptural verse or of reading it out of the Scriptural verse.

There is no space in this book to consider in detail all the material which we now have belonging to the *Halakhic Midrashim*. Instead the following selections are from the three main *Halakhic Midrashim* —*Mekhilta, Siphra* and *Siphre*. These three words are all Aramaic and mean: *Mekhilta*, "measure"; *Siphra*, "the book"; *Siphre*, "the books." The *Mekhilta* is a running commentary on the book of Exodus, the *Siphra* on the book of Leviticus, and the *Siphre* on the books of Numbers and Deuteronomy. (There is no *Halakhic Midrash* on Genesis because there is hardly any legal material in this book.)

The punishment for stealing

The different classes of stealing and their
appropriate punishments.

> When a man steals an ox or a sheep, and
> slaughters it or sells it, he shall pay five oxen
> for the ox, and four sheep for the sheep.
>
> EXODUS 21:37

The teachers mentioned in this passage belong to the
first (Johanan son of Zakkai) and the second centuries.

The slaughterer and the seller were already included in the verse:
"If the thief is caught, he shall pay double" (Exodus 22:6). But now
Scripture excludes these two cases from that general rule in order to
be stricter with them for they have to pay four or five times as much.
That is why this passage, Exodus 21:37, is recorded in the Torah.

Scripture says that a thief has to pay double the amount he had stolen
when he is caught. This rule would have embraced the case of the
thief who slaughters or sells the animal he has stolen. But Scripture
states this law separately to teach that for slaughtering and selling the
penalty is more severe and is four or five not merely double.

"An ox or a sheep"—to teach that he is to be punished for each of
them. "And slaughters it." I know only if he slaughters it, how do I

know that the same applies if he sells it? Because Scripture says: "or sells it." But even if Scripture did not state it explicitly I would have argued: If he is punished when he slaughters it, when he sells it he should certainly be punished. But if this were so you would have derived the punishment by an argument and therefore Scripture states explicitly: "or sells it," to teach you that one does not arrive at a legal punishment merely by means of an argument. Another explanation: Slaughtering is compared to selling and selling to slaughtering. Just as the penalty for selling only takes effect when he removes the animal from the domain of its owner so, too, the penalty of slaughtering only takes effect when he removes the animal from the domain of its owner. Further, just as the case of selling involves an animal which may be eaten, so too the case of slaughtering only applies to an animal which may be eaten. And just as the case of selling involves an animal from which it is permissible to have benefit, so too the case of slaughtering only applies to an animal from which one may have benefit. And conversely, just as the case of slaughtering cannot be undone, so too the penalty for selling is only when the sale is permanent. And just as the case of slaughtering is total, so too the case of selling only applies where the sale is total.

An ox or a sheep means that the penalty is for each and not only when he slaughtered or sold an ox and a sheep. The Mekhilta now argues that even if Scripture had not stated explicitly the case of selling I would have known that the penalty applies in this case, too. For surely a greater penalty should be given to the man who sells it and gains money thereby than to the man who slaughters it and gains no money. If, then, Scripture had simply recorded the case of slaughtering, we would know ourselves that the same penalty applies to the case of selling. Why then should Scripture have to state it explicitly? To this the answer is given that the case of selling is dealt with explicitly in Scripture to teach us that logical argument, strong though it is, should not be used as the sole basis for inflicting a penalty on someone. After all, one's argument, however convincing, may be mistaken. Consequently, Scripture is not content with giving us a basis for argument but states the law against selling explicitly. Another reason for Scripture stating both slaughtering and selling is then mentioned. This is so that we might compare the two and derive some new rules by the comparison. The principle here is that when Scripture compares two cases in the same verse it can logically be assumed that whatever is true of one case is also true of the other. The following examples are the particular points of comparison.

Obviously a man cannot be convicted of the crime of selling until he has actually sold what he has and he then removes it from its original owner's domain. Supposing a man slaughters his neighbor's animal while it is still on his neighbor's land? The comparison of slaughtering and selling is to teach that just as the law for selling the animal only applies when it has been removed from the owner's domain, so too the law for slaughtering. Furthermore, selling obviously involves an animal which may be eaten. For nowhere in Scripture do we find a law which states that an act of selling an animal renders it forbidden to eat or to have benefit from it. By the same token the law of slaughtering only applies if, after the slaughter, the animal can be eaten and benefit can be had from its meat. This excludes a diseased animal which is terefah—forbidden to be eaten—and an animal which killed a man, from which no benefit may be derived when it is slaughtered i.e. its meat must not be sold.

However just as slaughtering is compared to selling, so too selling is compared to slaughtering. A slaughtered animal cannot be brought back to life. The act is irrevocable. Supposing a man sold an animal for a short period i.e. he sold its use for thirty days. Such a sale would not warrant the penalty of four and five because it is not comparable to the irrevocable act of slaughtering. Similarly, one can only slaughter the whole of an animal not part of it. By the same token the penalty of four and five is only demanded where the whole of the animal was sold but not where a part of it was sold.

Another explanation: "When a man steals." You would think that animals set aside as Temple sacrifices are included in this law. So then if a man stole them from the Temple and slaughtered them outside the Temple area he must pay four or five. Scripture, however, in the book of Leviticus, makes an exception in the case of slaughtering Temple animals. It declares that in their case the penalty is a far stricter one than paying four or five and is that of being "cut off." Now one could have argued: If in the case of slaughtering Temple animals there is the stricter penalty of being cut off, how much more should it also include the lighter penalty of four and five? This is why Scripture says: "This is what the Lord hath commanded" (Leviticus

17:2). The law concerning Temple animals is the law of "cutting off." It is not the law of monetary restitution.

Leviticus 17:1-7 says that if a man slaughtered animals set aside for Temple sacrifices outside the Temple area he is to be punished with the penalty of being "cut off from his people." This means a kind of death sentence, not by the human court but at the hand of God at His own time and in His own way. The Mekhilta states here that one might have argued that in addition to the severe penalty of being cut off there is also the penalty of four and five. But in the passage dealing with Temple sacrifices slaughtered outside the Temple Scripture says: "This is what the Lord hath commanded," as if to say this penalty and no other in addition.

"He shall pay five oxen"—that is four and the original ox. "And four sheep"—that is three and the original sheep.

One might have understood the term "five" to mean five in addition to the value of the original animal and "four" to mean four in addition to the original animal. The Mekhilta states that this would hardly be the proper meaning of "four" and "five."

Rabbi Meir said: Come and see how much work is valued by God even though He brought the world into being by merely saying a word. The penalty for the ox which does work is five while the penalty of the sheep which does no work is only four. Rabbi Joḥanan son of Zakkai said: The Holy One, blessed be He, is concerned about the dignity of His creatures. In the case of an ox, which walks on its own, he has to pay five, but in the case of a sheep, which he has to carry, he only has to pay four.

The question now discussed is why should the thief have to pay more for an ox than for a sheep, why "five" for the ox and only "four" for the sheep? Two reasons are suggested. The ox is an animal which does work while the sheep is kept for its wool and mutton but not for its work. Scripture so values work that it always places a higher valuation on a working animal such as an ox. The second reason is that the thief when stealing the ox did not have to lower his dignity. But the thief when stealing a sheep had to carry it on his shoulder and this lowered his dignity. Scripture respects human dignity, even that of a thief, and therefore releases the man who stole the sheep from part of the payment because he has already been partly punished in his loss of dignity.

Rabbi Akiva said: "for the ox"—"for the sheep"—this is to exclude a beast of chase. For we might have argued that restitution has to be made when a domestic animal is stolen and restitution has to be made when a beast of chase is stolen. Therefore, it might have been argued, just as the restitution in the one case involves the penalty of four or five, so, too, in the other case. No, the two cases are unlike one another, for the domestic animal can be offered on the Temple altar as a sacrifice but the beast of chase cannot be offered on the altar so it does not warrant the penalty of four or five. But a domestic animal with a blemish which cannot be offered on the altar still warrants the penalty of four and five! This would be an argument to warrant the penalty of four and five for the beast of chase even though it cannot be offered on the altar. No, even though a domestic animal with a blemish cannot be offered on the altar it belongs to a species which can, whereas the beast of chase cannot as a species be offered on the altar. Scripture therefore says: "for the ox"—"for the sheep"— and excludes the beast of chase.

A "beast of chase" is an animal such as a deer. These may be eaten but were never offered on the altar in the Temple. On the basis of this the argument is developed to exclude them from special penalty. To make absolutely sure of this according to Rabbi Akiva, Scripture states "for the ox"—"for the sheep"—to suggest only for these.

Moral human relations

The laws of living with others ethically.

> Ye shall not steal; neither shall ye deal falsely, nor lie to
> one another. And ye shall not swear by My name falsely,
> so that thou profane the name of thy God: I am the Lord.
> Thou shalt not oppress thy neighbor, nor rob him; the
> wages of a hired servant shall not abide with thee all night
> until the morning. Thou shalt not curse the deaf, nor
> put a stumbling block before the blind, but thou shalt
> fear thy God: I am the Lord.
>
> LEVITICUS 19:11—14

**"Ye shall not steal." Why is this stated? Because Scripture states with
regard to theft that the thief has to pay double (Exodus 22:3). That
is the penalty. How do we know of the prohibition? Therefore
Scripture says here: "Ye shall not steal."**

*The Rabbis believed that Scripture nowhere states a penalty for
an offense unless it also somewhere warns Israel against
committing the offense.*

**"Ye shall not steal." This applies even if you steal only for the purpose
of causing the victim anxiety; or if your intention is to pay double
or four or five. Ben Bag Bag says: Do not even steal back from a thief
that which he has stolen from you lest you appear to be a thief.**

The Siphra *interprets the commandment to include cases of theft which are still forbidden even though they might not be considered as real cases of theft. For instance, supposing a man steals, not to keep that which he has stolen, but simply to make the victim anxious and to return the stolen goods eventually; this is still theft and forbidden. Or take the law that if a thief is caught he has to pay double the amount or if he slaughters or sells an ox or a sheep that he has stolen he has to pay four or five times as much. Supposing, then, a man steals in order to benefit the victim by letting him have either double or four or five times the value eventually? The Siphra rules that this, too, is forbidden. Ben Bag Bag was a first century Palestinian teacher. (Some suggest that he was a convert to Judaism and that his curious name is to be explained in this manner: Bag is formed of the letters bet and gimmel which equals two and three. Now "five" is the letter hé which was added to the names of Abraham and Sarah. Hence, since a convert to Judaism is said to be the "son of Abraham and Sarah" he would have been called Ben (the son of) Bag Bag. In fact, there is another teacher of the same period called Ben Hé Hé!) According to Ben Bag Bag it is forbidden to steal even from a thief and even that which the thief has himself stolen. If a man can identify his property he should bring the case before the courts and not take the law into his own hands. Authorities in the Talmud in a later generation said, however, that if there is no possibility of getting redress in the courts then he may take the law into his own hands and steal his own property back from the thief.*

"Ye shall not steal: neither shall ye deal falsely." Why is this stated? Because when Scripture says: "And deal falsely therein" (Leviticus 5:22) we are told the penalty (restitution plus a one-fifth penalty; Leviticus 5:24), but how do we know the prohibition? Therefore Scripture says here: "Ye shall not steal; nor lie to one another."

See the comment on the first paragraph.

"To one another" ("a man to his neighbor"). I only learn that it applies to a man offending against a man. What if a man offends against a woman? Therefore Scripture says "his neighbor" to include everyone.

Obviously the term "man" is not intended to exclude the application of the law to women. A woman is just as much a fellow-citizen, a "neighbor," as a man.

"Ye shall not steal; neither shall ye deal falsely, nor lie to one another. And ye shall not swear by My name falsely." Which means that if you do steal you will eventually deal falsely and eventually lie and eventually swear falsely.

This explains itself. The Siphra takes each of the offenses recorded as leading on to the others.

"And ye shall not swear by My name falsely." Why is this stated? Because Scripture states: "Thou shalt not take the name of the Lord thy God in vain" (Exodus 20:7). From this I might have argued that the penalty only applies when the special Divine name has been used. How do we know that it applies to any of the other names of God? Therefore Scripture states here: "And ye shall not swear by My name" which means by any name I have.

The "special Divine name" is the four-letter name translated as Lord. In the third of the Ten Commandments this is the term used. Hence the Siphra states that it might have been argued that the full penalty is only where this special name is used. But since in our verse there is simply a reference to "My name" it includes any name by which God is known e.g. God, Almighty, and so forth.

"So that thou profane the name of thy God." This teaches us that a false oath is a profanation of God's name. Another explanation: if you swear falsely your life becomes profane to the wild beasts.

Scripture says: "And ye shall not profane My holy name; but I shall be hallowed among the children of Israel" (Leviticus 22:32). The rabbis say that there are two ideas here: 1) The avoidance of Ḥillul Ha-Shem (the profanation of the Name); 2) Kiddush Ha-Shem (the sanctification of the Name). Ḥillul Ha-Shem means to do anything which brings religion into disrepute e.g. if a man so behaves that people despise him and the religion he adheres to because it has not succeeded in making him a better

person. Kiddush Ha-Shem *means behaving so well that people say:
If this is the kind of person the religion produces it must
be supremely worthwhile. The second explanation here is rather
difficult. It is probably based on the idea that while God has
ordered the animals, as it were, to refrain from harming man, when
men sin He does allow the animals to do harm. Furthermore when
man sins he causes the world to be devastated and he cannot
build a civilized life.*

**It is in reference to this that Scripture says: "Therefore hath a curse
devoured the earth, and they that dwell therein are found guilty;
Therefore the inhabitants of the earth waste away, and men are left
few" (Isaiah 24:6).**

*A verse from Isaiah is quoted in support of what has been said
in the previous comment.*

**"Thou shalt not oppress thy neighbor." It might have been argued
that this applies also to someone who says of a certain man that he
is not powerful when in reality he is, or that he is not wise when in
reality he is, or that he is not rich when in reality he is. Scripture
therefore says "nor rob him." Just as robbery refers to a case where
money is involved, so too oppressing refers to a case where money
is involved. Which case is that? Keeping back the wages of a hired
servant. "The wages of a hired servant shall not abide with thee all
night until the morning." I know only that the law applies to the
wages of a human being. How do we know that it also applies to the
rental fee of an animal or of vessels or of land? Scripture therefore
says "Shall not abide with thee" to include anything for which
payment is due.**

*The beginning of this paragraph is not at all clear in the original
text. Our translation follows the suggested reading of the
famous scholar, the Gaon of Vilna (eighteenth century). The meaning
is that the full penalty of theft only applies to theft of money
or property, not to the theft of a man's reputation. This is, of
course, a legal distinction. Morally to rob a man of his reputation
may be much worse but such theft is difficult to put right in
a court of law.
The second part of this paragraph states that any wages owed to*

a person falls under the law of keeping back wages, even wages
for the hire of tools or land or other property.

"Until the morning." This teaches that he does not offend against the law until the first morning after the work has been done. I might have supposed that the law applies even when the hired servant did not demand his wages. Therefore Scripture says "with thee." I only object, says God, to wages you hold back of your own free will.

This paragraph states two things. First that he has the whole night
to pay and does not offend against the law until the morning.
Secondly, if the hired workman does not mind being owed the
money and does not claim it right away, his employer commits
no offense if he does not pay him right away. This is derived from
the words "with thee" which suggest that the employer keeps
the money back when requested by the workman.

I might have supposed that the law applies even where he gave the workman credit at a bank or a shop. Therefore Scripture says "with thee"—it only applies if the wages were kept back willingly.

Since the offense is only where the employer willfully intended to
postpone payment it does not apply if, instead of money, he
gave him credit at a bank and at a shop i.e. to buy goods there
for his needs and charge the bill to the employer. The giving of the
credit note then becomes the payment of the wages. Jewish law
has it, however, that he may only do this with the consent of the
employee, otherwise he must give him money not goods.

"The wages of a hired servant shall not abide with thee until the morning." From this I learn only that a man engaged to work by day has all the night to demand his wages. How do we know that a man who works at night has all the next day to demand his wages? Therefore Scripture says: "In the same day thou shalt give him his hire" (Deuteronomy 24:15).

The point here is that there are two verses in Scripture regarding
the hired workman. One deals with a man hired for work
during the day and he must be paid the next night. The other deals
with a man hired to work during the night and he must be paid the
next day.

"Thou shalt not curse the deaf." I know only that it is forbidden to curse a deaf man. How do we know that it is forbidden to curse any man? Therefore Scripture says: "Nor curse a ruler of thy people" (Exodus 22:27). If that is so why is a deaf man specified? To teach you that the law only applies to one who is like the deaf man, namely one who is alive. But the law does not apply to the dead.

The plain meaning of the verse is that it is forbidden to curse even a deaf man who cannot hear the curse. But it might have been argued that it is only forbidden to do this to one who cannot hear and cannot retaliate. Therefore the Siphra proves that it applies to others as well since there is another verse forbidding the cursing of a ruler. The principle here is that since a ruler and a deaf man are mentioned and are so different, Scripture intends the prohibition to apply to that which both have in common, namely their humanity. It follows that the law applies then to every human being. The Siphra takes the two verses together as meaning that it is forbidden to curse anyone, but that the two cases of ruler and deaf man are specially singled out. The paragraph concludes that when one speaks of a deaf man one must be speaking of a living person who is deaf but has his other faculties. The term would not be used of a dead man. Consequently, the Siphra rules that the full prohibition does not apply to anyone who curses a dead man. Many people think that it is worse to speak ill of the dead than of the living, as in the Latin tag: "de mortuis nil nisi bonum." But the Siphra holds that it is far worse to speak evil of the living, who can be harmed, than of the dead who cannot be harmed by anything we say of them.

"Nor put a stumbling-block before the blind." This means before someone who is blind to a certain thing. If for example, a man asks you whether the daughter of so-and-so may marry a priest, you must not tell him that she may when in reality she may not. If a man asks your advice do not give him harmful advice. Do not tell him to get up early in the morning in order that he might be captured by bandits or go out at noontime so that he might suffer sun-stroke. Do not advise him to sell his field and buy a donkey in order to seek an opportunity to get it for yourself. You might argue: I am giving him good advice. But the thing is known in the heart, as it is said: "but thou shalt fear thy God; I am the Lord."

The Siphra argues that the verse can be extended to anyone who is blind to a mistake he is making. He should not be encouraged to persist in his mistake. You must not take advantage of his weakness for your own gain or to vent your malice on him. Certain people were forbidden to a priest—a divorced woman, for example. If a priest asks you whether he should propose to a girl, and he only wishes to do so if he knows that he may marry her, you must not cause pain to both of them by misleading him. The other examples explain themselves. The final comment is to the effect that while a man can fool his neighbors God knows of it and He cannot be fooled.

Safety first

The law of making the roof of one's house safe.

> When thou buildest a new house, thou shalt make a parapet for thy roof, so that thou bring not blood-guilt upon thy house if anyone should fall from it.
>
> DEUTERONOMY 22:8

"When thou buildest a new house." I know only that the law applies when he builds a house. How do we know that it applies also when he buys a house or inherits one or when a house is given to him as a gift? Therefore Scripture says "so that thou bring not bloodguilt upon thy house" and this covers all cases. I know only a proper house. How do we know that the law applies also to a place in which straw is kept or to a stable or to a place in which wood is kept or to any other kind of storehouse? Therefore Scripture says "so that thou bring not bloodguilt upon thy house" and this covers all cases. In that case we might have supposed that the law applies also to a lodge at the gate or to a balcony or to a porch, therefore Scripture speaks of "a house." A house means a place used for living in, but these are not in constant use.

The Siphre *argues against a too literal interpretation of the word "build." Since the reason given for making a parapet is to protect people from falling, it obviously makes no difference whether the* house is one newly built or whether bought, received as a gift or inherited. If it has no parapet it is the duty of the owner to make one. The laws here refer to houses with flat roofs since these were often used by people for workspace or pleasure. They were dangerous without proper protection from falling. The Rabbis in the Talmud extend the law developed here to include all manner of dangerous things. They said, for example, that a man must not keep an unstable ladder in his house or a vicious dog. In the Siphre, however, the law is said not to extend to mere casual rooms which are hardly ever used, like the porch at a gateway. One would not normally go up onto the roof of such a place. The reference to the balcony is to the roof of the balcony.

"Thou shalt make a parapet for thy roof." I know only that the law applies to a roof. How do we know that it also applies to a pit or a well or a dug-out or a cellar? Therefore Scripture says "so that thou bring not bloodguilt upon thy house" and this covers all cases. If that is so why does it say a "roof?" This is to exclude the ramp to the altar in the Temple. Furthermore, the term "house" includes the Temple itself but the term "roof" excludes the entrance hall of the Temple.

The Siphre goes on to say that the term "roof" must not be taken too literally. If a man had an underground dwelling into which people could fall he is similarly obliged to build a protecting wall around it. But then why mention a "roof"? The Siphre replies that this is to indicate that the ramp leading to the altar in the Temple did not require a protective rail. This may be because the priests who used the ramp were careful where they walked and were used to it. The Temple is called a "house"—the house of God—and hence a parapet should be made around its roof. But the excluding term "roof" meaning the roof of a house suggests that a parapet is not required around the entrance hall of the Temple, probably because it was unusual for anyone but the priests and Levites to walk there and, again, they were used to it.

"New." Rabbi says: Make the parapet while the house is new. How high should the parapet be? If the roof is only used for rolling the earth (to keep out the rain) it need be no higher than three hand-breadths, but if the roof is used for human beings to walk on

regularly it must be at least ten handbreadths high. "Thou shalt make a parapet." This is a positive commandment. "So that thou bring not bloodguilt upon thy house." This is a negative commandment.

"New." This term is interpreted by Rabbi (Rabbi Judah the Prince, the editor of the Mishnah, who, because of his importance, is simply called "Rabbi" without his name being added) to mean that it is a religious duty to build the parapet as soon as one builds the house, not to wait until the house is old to some extent. If the roof is only resorted to for the purpose of keeping everything in order only a small protective wall is required, otherwise a better protective wall is called for.

"If anyone should fall from it." The man who falls deserves to do so but good things are brought about by good people and bad things by bad people.

This is an interesting comment. It is based on the fact that the Hebrew of the verse can mean "the fallen one should fall from it." The interpretation is given that God would not let man fall unless He had so ordained it. In that case why is the person who neglected to build the parapet to blame? The man would have fallen in any event. Yes, answers the Siphre, but the good person should never be the instrument of God in such a matter. The question raised here is a very important one. Some people argue that it does not matter so much if accidents are caused by one's negligence because if God does not want the accident to happen He will not allow it. This passage in the Siphre reminds us that this is an irreligious attitude. God has given human beings the skills and wisdom to care for life and this is their duty.

"From it." And not *into* it. If the public domain were ten hand-breadths higher than the house and someone fell *into* the house the owner of the house is not guilty, as it is said: "from it" and not "into it."

Although even in this case it would obviously be a good thing for the man to build a parapet, he does not incur any guilt if he fails to do so.

The Mishnah

IN OUR note on the *Halakhic Midrashim* we remarked that the Midrash process is to connect a law with a Scriptural verse. Side by side with this process there was another in which the law arrived at was presented on its own (i.e. without reference to a verse). Such a statement of a law in concise form was known as a Mishnah (meaning a "teaching"). The plural of Mishnah is Mishnayot. In the course of time many thousands of Mishnayot were known in the great Palestinian schools of learning.

We have already referred, in the note to the *Halakhic Midrashim*, to the *Tannaim*, the great teachers of the first and second centuries in Palestine. In their schools were taught and handed down from generation to generation both the Midrashim and the Mishnayot. There were a number of Mishnayot collections e.g. from the School of Rabbi Akiva and the School of his pupil Rabbi Meir in the second century. Eventually the famous leader of his people, Rabbi Judah the Prince, edited all the Mishnaic material which had accumulated and put the material into shape in the form of six "Orders"—the Six Orders of the Mishnah. Each order is divided into tractates (known as *Massekhtot*, singular *Massekhet*, an Aramaic word meaning a "web") and each tractate into chapters. Each chapter is in turn divided into smaller units called Mishnayot. The term Mishnah is thus at one and the same time the name of the smallest unit and the name of the work as a whole.

The Mishnah as edited by Rabbi Judah the Prince around the year 200 of the present era became the authoritative statement of Jewish law then. Rabbi Judah the Prince did not include all the material of the Tannaitic period but was selective. He did not include, for instance, all the Rabbis' studies in traditions which we now have in the Halakhic Midrashim. Much of what he did not include was, of course, well known in his day. A Tannaitic statement of law that was "outside" i.e. not incorporated into, the Mishnah, is sometimes referred to as a Baraita, plural Baraitot (from a root meaning "to be outside"). Later teachers frequently rely on Baraitot in order to elucidate the teachings of the Mishnah. There is also a work known as the Tosephta (the word means "supplement") which is a collection of Baraitot dating from the Tannaitic period. It does not have the authority of the Mishnah but it is an important auxiliary help in later Jewish legal discussions.

Thus the main forms in which the teachings of the Tannaim are to be found are: 1) The Halakhic Midrashim (3 books); 2) The Baraitot (quoted by later teachers but nowhere presented systematically); 3) The Tosephta (a more systematic collection in book form; 4) The Mishnah. 1, 2 and 3 are all technically Baraitot (though usually the term is reserved for 2 while the others are called by their particular name).

The Mishnah in its six orders covers the whole range of Jewish law. Thus the first order deals with all the laws regarding agriculture; the second with Sabbaths and Festivals; the third with marriage and divorce; the fourth with civil law proper, such as damages and theft; the fifth with the Temple and sacrifices; and the sixth with the laws which obtained in Temple times, of purity and impurity. The Hebrew names of the six orders are:

1. Zeraim	— Seeds	4. Nezikin	— Damages
2. Moed	— Festivals	5. Kodashim	— Sacred Things
3. Nashim	— Women	6. Tohorot	— Pure Things

It should be noted that almost the whole of 5 and 6 no longer had any practical application after the destruction of the Temple in the year 70, about a century and a half before the Mishnah was edited.

Nevertheless Rabbi Judah the Prince included these rules of *Kodashim* and *Tohorot* because his aim was to give the most complete possible picture of the law.

It remains to be said that the Mishnah was compiled in a lucid Hebrew, which, incidentally, has had a great deal of influence on modern spoken and written Hebrew. Although Aramaic was widely spoken in Palestine during the period of the *Tannaim,* the scholarly language was still Hebrew. Hence both the Mishnah and the various Baraitot are in Hebrew.

CHAPTER 4

Making arrangements on the Sabbath

The arrangements which do and do not infringe upon proper Sabbath observance.

A man may borrow jars of wine and jars of oil from his neighbor on the Sabbath but he should not say: "Lend me." A woman may similarly borrow from her neighbor loaves of bread. If one of them does not trust the other, the borrower may leave his cloak (as a pledge) and reckon it up after the Sabbath. Similarly, in Jerusalem, when the eve of Passover falls on Sabbath, a man may leave his cloak with the dealer from whom he has obtained the paschal lamb and reckon it up with him after the Festival.

The principle here is that it is wrong to do anything on the Sabbath which looks like business dealings. Consequently, while it is permitted to borrow jars of wine and oil and pay for them after the Sabbath, it is not permitted to say "lend me these" for this kind of expression is the one generally used in commercial transactions. Suppose the lender does not trust the borrower? Then the borrower may leave his cloak or some other object of value as a pledge and after the Sabbath the amount owing will be reckoned up. The point here is that leaving the cloak as a pledge does not look too much like a business transaction but to make a detailed reckoning of the cost does. In Jerusalem in Temple times it sometimes happened that the eve of Passover (when the paschal lamb had to be brought to the Temple) fell on the Sabbath. Supposing a man had forgotten to buy his paschal lamb? He is allowed to purchase one from a dealer but should not go into the question of price. If the dealer does not trust him he should leave his cloak as a pledge.

A man may reckon up the number of his guests and the choice portions to be served provided that he does it by word of mouth but not from a written document. He may cast lots among his children and the other members of his household for the various portions, but he should not intend to have the lots decide which person is to receive a large portion and which a small for this would be like playing dice for money on the Sabbath. Lots may be cast in the Temple for the Hallowed Things (from the sacrifices offered on the Festivals) but not from the portions (of the sacrifices offered before the Festivals).

It was the custom at large banquets in those days for the host to have a list of the guests and also of the special dainties he was to serve. When checking these on the Sabbath the host should do it all by heart and should not rely on a documented list as he does on a weekday for he may easily forget that it is the Sabbath and make alterations in writing on the list.

It appears that it was customary for the head of the household to cast lots to decide which of the members of the family was to have which portion and who was to be served first and the like. This is permitted even on the Sabbath. But it is not permitted to play off a large portion against a smaller one for then the winner gains a portion of greater value and this is as if they were playing dice for money.

In Temple times the meat of some sacrifices went to the priests. They are permitted to cast lots to decide who is to have which portion but this is only permitted with regard to sacrifices offered up on the Festival. It is not permitted if the sacrifices had been offered up before the Festival for in this case they should have cast the lots then and not left it until the Festival.

A man should not hire workmen on the Sabbath or say to his neighbor that he should hire workmen for him. A man may not go to await nightfall at the Sabbath boundary for the purpose of hiring workmen or bringing back fruit, but he may go to await nightfall there for the purpose of protecting the fruit and then there is no objection to him bringing the fruit back with him. Abba Saul laid down this rule: I am permitted to await nightfall for those things I am allowed to speak about on the Sabbath.

To hire workmen is a business transaction forbidden on the Sabbath even if no money changes hands. It is even forbidden to ask a friend to hire workmen, although the friend may do this after the Sabbath. The Sabbath boundary is a line around a city extending 2,000 cubits (just over half a mile). Beyond this it is forbidden to walk on the Sabbath. The question the Mishnah here considers is whether it is permitted to walk to the boundary on the Sabbath so as to be ready to go beyond it as soon as night falls. The Mishnah rules that it is permitted to do this in order to be ready to protect his fruit but not for hiring workmen or bringing back the fruit. However, if he went there in order to protect the fruit and then, after the Sabbath, decided to bring back some fruit it is permitted since he did not go there with that intention. The second century Palestinian teacher Abba Saul explains the difference by a rule. It is forbidden to hire workmen or to bring fruit from outside the boundary on the Sabbath. Consequently it is forbidden to await nightfall for this purpose. But it is permitted to sit beside fruit growing in the field to protect the fruit and therefore it is permitted to await nightfall for this purpose. Hence Abba Saul's rule: If I am permitted to speak about a thing on the Sabbath (I may say to someone: Please protect my fruit) I am allowed to await nightfall for it. But if I am not permitted to speak about something on the Sabbath (I may not say to someone: Hire workmen for me or bring fruit to me from outside the boundary) I am not allowed to await nightfall for it.

It is permitted to await nightfall for the purposes of arranging for a wedding reception or for a corpse, to fetch its coffin and shrouds. If a gentile brought flutes on the Sabbath a Jew must not play dirges on them unless they came from a place nearby. If a grave had been dug or a coffin made for a gentile, a Jew may be buried in it. But if it had been made for a Jew no Jew may ever be buried in it.

Even though according to the general rule it is not permitted to await nightfall for purposes which may not be carried out on the Sabbath, the Mishnah here states that the Rabbis made two exceptions. The first is for the purpose of arranging a wedding feast.

This is a great religious duty and so an exception was made. The second is for another important religious duty, that of burying the dead in a fitting manner.

It was the custom in those days to play dirges at a funeral. The Mishnah rules that even if a gentile (who is, of course, not obliged to keep the Jewish Sabbath) brought the flutes for this purpose from outside the boundary on the Sabbath, it is forbidden to use the flutes even after the Sabbath at the funeral. But if they came from a place nearby, i.e. from within the Sabbath boundary, it is permitted. If the gentile had made ready a coffin or a grave without intending it for a Jew, it is permitted for a Jew to use it. But if the grave had been specially prepared for a Jew on the Sabbath then it is forbidden for a Jew to use it. He may not gain the benefit of forbidden work done on the Sabbath (even though it is not forbidden for the gentile to do the work):

It is permitted to do all that is necessary for a corpse, washing it and anointing it for example, provided that no limb of the corpse is moved. It is permitted to take away the mattress from under a corpse in order to preserve the corpse by letting it lie on the sand. It is permitted to bind up the chin, not in order to close the jaw but so that it should not open wider. Similarly it is permitted to prop up a rafter which has broken with a bench or the side pieces of a bed, not in order to elevate it but in order that it may not split further. It is forbidden to close the eyes of a corpse on the Sabbath. Even on the weekday it is forbidden to close the eyes of a man who is about to die. Whoever closes the eyes of a man who is about to die is a shedder of blood.

It is permitted to make a corpse ready for burial. However, the Mishnah rules that it is forbidden to move any limb of the corpse. The idea here is that a corpse, or for that matter anything not generally in use, should not be moved on the Sabbath. Certain exceptions are however recorded.

It was the custom to close the eyes of a dead person. Since this is only a custom it may not be done on the Sabbath. Even on a weekday it is forbidden to close the eyes of a man who is about to die. The principle here is that any such movement may hasten the end and even though the man will die in any event it is wrong to deprive him of any extra minutes of life he may have.

What do vows cover?

*The different ways in which a man can prohibit
certain benefits to himself.*

*Although, generally speaking, the Rabbis discouraged the taking of
vows, if a man solemnly took a vow to abstain from certain things or
to have no benefit from certain persons he is obliged to keep his
word. In all the passages quoted the basic question is one of
definition. What is covered by this or that term? What is the scope
of the vow? To "have benefit" means to obtain any gain or pleasure
from a thing or person i.e. to drink wine or to receive a gift
from someone.*

**If a man vowed that he would have no benefit from sea-farers he is
permitted to have benefit from dwellers on land. But if he vowed
that he would have no benefit from dwellers on land he must not
have any benefit even from sea-farers, since sea-farers are included
in the term "dwellers on land." The term "sea-farers" does not apply
to those who merely go by sea from Acre to Jaffa but only to those
who sail for distant parts.**

*A man, who perhaps hated the sea, took a vow that he would have
no benefit from sea-farers. The Mishnah rules that the term does not
include anyone who may take a sea voyage but only those who have
actually done so. Consequently he is permitted to have benefit*

from dwellers on land. But if his vow covered dwellers on land this term would include all men, since even sea-farers do eventually come back to land. The Mishnah adds that the term "sea-farers" is generally used for those who journey by sea from one country to another. But those who take a trip by boat from Acre, in the north of Palestine, to Jaffa lower down on the same sea coast, are not included. In our parlance, too, a person who goes on a small pleasure cruise at the sea-side is hardly called a sailor.

If a man vowed that he would have no benefit from those who see the sun he is forbidden to have benefit also from the blind since his intention was from those whom the sun sees.

The term "those who see the sun" must not be taken literally so as to exclude blind persons who cannot see. The term simply means those who dwell on earth, i.e. all men on whom the sun shines.

If a man vowed to have no benefit from black-haired people he is forbidden to have benefit also from bald-headed and grey-haired people. But he may have benefit from women and children since only grown-up men are referred to as black-haired.

In the times of the Mishnah the term "black-haired" never referred to women and children. On the other hand it was never taken literally so as to exclude men with grey hair or bald men without any hair at all.

If a man vowed that he would have no benefit from people that are born he is permitted to have benefit from those yet unborn. But if he vowed to have no benefit from those to be born he is forbidden also to have benefit from those already born. Rabbi Meir permits it also with regard to those already born. But the Sages say that this man only intended to mean those species who bring forth young.

The point in this Mishnah is that the term "those that are born" does exclude those still to be born so that if a man took such a vow for many years he will eventually be permitted to have benefit from those born after his vow. But the term "those who are to be born" means in Hebrew all people who are born. In fact, it would include all creatures, including animals, who give birth directly to their young, and would only exclude fishes and birds.

If a man vows to have no benefit from "those who keep the Sabbath" he is forbidden to have benefit both from Jews and from Samaritans. If he vows to have no benefit from "those who eat garlic" he is forbidden to have benefit from both Jews and Samaritans. If a man vows to have no benefit from "those who go up to Jerusalem" he is forbidden to have benefit from Jews but he may have benefit from Samaritans.

The Samaritans were a sect, with its headquarters on Mount Gerizim, who claimed to be Jews but who were viewed with suspicion by the Rabbis. They kept many of the Jewish laws and certainly observed the Sabbath. They even observed certain minor Jewish customs such as that of eating garlic on the Sabbath. Thus the terms "those who keep the Sabbath" and "those who eat garlic" include the Samaritans. But the Samaritans did not go on pilgrimage to Jerusalem, hence the term "those who go up to Jerusalem" does not include them.

If a man vowed that he would have no benefit from milk he is permitted to have benefit from whey, but Rabbi José forbids it. If he vows to have no benefit from whey he is permitted to have benefit from milk. Abba Saul says that if a man vows to have no benefit from cheese he is forbidden to have benefit from cheese whether it is salted or unsalted.

Curds and whey are not included in the term "milk." If a man vows that he will have no benefit from milk it can be assumed that he means milk itself and not any of its products. But Rabbi José argues that his intention was to include milk products as well. Even Rabbi José would agree, however, that the term "whey" would not include milk. Cheese was normally salted before use. Nevertheless Abba Saul argues that salted or unsalted the term "cheese" can be said to embrace it.

If a man vows to have no benefit from meat he is permitted to have benefit from meat-soup or meat-sediment, but Rabbi Judah forbids it. Rabbi Judah said: It once happened that I took such a vow and Rabbi Tarphon refused to allow me to eat even eggs that had been cooked with the meat. The Sages replied: Yes that was so but it only applies to someone who declared: "This specific piece of meat is forbidden to me." For then the law is that whoever vows to abstain from something and it is mixed with something else so that it gives that thing flavor, the thing, too, is forbidden.

The man who vows to abstain from meat, the Sages argue, means to include in the term only the meat itself but not dishes in which there is a meat flavor. Rabbi Judah disagrees and forbids even a meat flavor. Rabbi Judah seeks to prove his case by a reference to the ruling of his teacher Rabbi Tarphon but the Sages make a clear distinction. If a general vow of abstinence from meat is made, it embraces only meat and not dishes with a meat flavor. But if a particular piece of meat had been placed under a ban by a vow then this piece of meat, being forbidden, has the power of contaminating, as it were, any dishes in which it imparted a flavor.

If a man vowed to have no benefit from wine he is permitted to enjoy a dish which has wine flavoring. But if he said: "This wine is forbidden to me" and the wine fell into a dish, that dish is forbidden to him if the wine flavor can be tasted. If a man vows that he will have no benefit from grapes he may have benefit from wine; that he will have no benefit from olives he may have benefit from olive oil. If he said: "These olives and grapes are forbidden to me" both they and whatever comes from them are forbidden to him.

This paragraph follows on the rule in the previous one. If he forswears some particular wine, it contaminates any dishes to which it imparts a flavor; but if only a general vow were taken to abstain from wine it can be assumed that the term "wine" does not embrace dishes in which there is wine flavor. Similarly, the terms "grapes" and "olives" do not embrace the products of these (wine and olive oil). But if he swore not to touch particular grapes or particular olives then whatever comes from them is forbidden.

If a man vowed that he would have no benefit from dates, he is permitted to enjoy date-honey. If he vowed to have no benefit from winter grapes, he is permitted to enjoy vinegar made from winter grapes. Rabbi Judah son of Betayra says: If a man vowed to abstain from something which is called by the name of its product he is forbidden to enjoy the product as well, but the Sages permit it.

Two further examples of how a general vow does not include the products: Honey made from dates is not embraced by the term "dates" and vinegar made from winter grapes is not embraced by the term "winter-grapes." Rabbi Judah dissents here because, he argues, dates are sometimes called "honey" and winter-grapes are sometimes called "vinegar."

If a man vowed that he would have no benefit from wine, he may enjoy wine made from apples; that he would have no benefit from oil, he may have sesame oil; that he would have no benefit from honey, he may have date-honey; that he would have no benefit from vinegar, he may have vinegar made from winter grapes; that he would have no benefit from leeks, he may have shallots; that he would have no benefit from vegetables, he may have wild vegetables, since these have a special name.

Wine generally means grape-wine, not apple wine; oil generally means olive oil, not sesame oil; honey generally means from bees, not from dates; vinegar generally means from wine that has become sour, not from winter grapes; leeks are not generally used as a term for shallots; and vegetables do not normally include wild vegetables, because these have the special name "wild vegetables."

CHAPTER 6

MISHNAH, BAVA METZIA, CHAPTERS 1:1–2; 3:3–5

To whom does it belong?

The settlement of conflicting claims of ownership.

Two men are holding a cloak; This one says: "I found it" and the other one says: "I found it." If this one says: "It is all mine" and the other one says: "It is all mine"—then this one must swear that he does not own less than a half and the other one must swear that he does not own less than a half and they divide it. If this one says: "It is all mine" and the other one says: "Half of it is mine"—then the one who says "It is all mine" must swear that he does not own less than three quarters and the one who says: "Half of it is mine" must swear that he does not own less than a quarter and this one takes three quarters and this one takes one quarter.

The first case is where two men come before the court each claiming ownership of a cloak. Each one claims that he was the one who found the cloak. (Normally a cloak that is found must be returned to its owner. In this hypothetical case either the garment was found in such circumstances that it is clear it has been abandoned by its owner or all efforts to find the owner have proved futile, in which case it belongs to the finder). Now if one of the men were holding the cloak and the other merely trailing along behind him, the one actually holding the cloak would be allowed to keep it. He has possession and "possession is nine points of the law." But here both of them are holding the cloak, neither of them having a greater claim on it than the other. Now what is to be done in such a case?

Now the law could have decided that since there is no way of discovering which of the two is telling the truth the cloak should be divided between them, each receiving a half or its value. But if this were done, justice would not be satisfied since each of them claims the whole of the cloak and to give each a half would certainly be to perpetrate an act of injustice in giving a half belonging to the rightful owner to the trickster. Consequently, the Mishnah rules that each of them must swear that he is telling the truth. The general principle is that while a man may be willing to tell an untruth in order to obtain something that is not his, he will be reluctant to swear in court that he is telling the truth when he is not really doing so. The purpose of the oath is to persuade the trickster to admit he is telling an untruth. But, rules the Mishnah, if both of them do take the oath then there is nothing for the court to do but to give each of them a half of its value.

The Gemara (the later commentary to the Mishnah) explains that actually each of them should swear that he owns the whole of it. Why then the peculiar form of swearing: "I do not own less than a half"? If each one were to swear that he owns all of it and the court could only then give each a half, it would be a kind of public discredit of the court so openly to contradict the words of the oath. As it is each of them only states on oath openly that he owns at least a half. But the Gemara objects that in such a case the trickster can swear "I do not own less than a half" while in his heart he can say: "I do not own less than a half i.e. I do not own any of it, therefore I do not own less than a half." To this the answer is given that he must swear: "I do own something of this cloak and that which I own is not less than a half."

The second case of the Mishnah is more complicated. One of the two men claims that he found the cloak and it is consequently all his, but the other claims that they both found it together and that, therefore, each owns a half. Since one of them admits that a half belongs certainly to the other, the point at dispute is over the other half. This half is then treated as the whole cloak in the first case so that one swears that he owns three quarters i.e. the half admitted to be his and a half of the rest and the other swears that he owns a quarter. (Actually, as in the first case, they swear that they own not less than three quarters and not less than a quarter respectively.)

The second half of the cloak is then divided between them, this one receiving three quarters of the total value, the other a quarter.

If two men were riding on an animal or one was riding and one was leading the animal: This one says: "It is all mine" and the other one says: "It is all mine"—then this one must swear that he does not own less than a half and the other one must swear that he does not own less than a half and they divide it.

If they both agree or they both have witnesses they divide it without an oath.

This case of the Mishnah concerns a claim to an animal. Actually this, in principle, is exactly the same as the first case. The Gemara suggests that it is repeated to teach that rider and leader of the animal have equal claims to possession, otherwise we might have thought that the rider, for example, is treated as the man in possession and the leader simply has no claim. When it says that the animal is divided it does not, of course, mean that the animal has to be killed and cut up (any more than the division of the cloak in the first case means that the cloak must be cut in two) but its value is divided between them.

The final clause of the Mishnah states that, of course, all this is where there are no means for the court to decide where the truth lies. But if they themselves eventually admit that they found it together or where each of them produces witnesses that he found it, then the court simply orders the cloak to be divided without subjecting them to an oath.

It might have been argued in the case where both of them produce witnesses that he alone found it that an oath be taken, since the witnesses to the claims of one are obviously false witnesses. But the point here is that we do not find in Jewish law anywhere the suggestion that an oath be taken where there are witnesses. To demand an oath in such cases would have the effect of weakening the testimony of witnesses in other cases. Consequently, the general principle is adhered to that there must be no oath where there are witnesses.

A man said to two others: I know that I have stolen a *maneh* (one hundred *zuz*) from one of you but I do not know from which one

of you. Or he says: The father of one of you deposited a *maneh* with me but I do not know to which of you it belongs. He must give a *maneh* to this one and a *maneh* to the other one since he himself had admitted it.

In the first case of the Mishnah a man admits that he owes one of two men a sum of money but he cannot recall which of them. He knows for certain that it is one of these two and they themselves cannot throw any light on the matter. Since he admits to having a maneh which belongs to someone else and he wishes to satisfy his conscience, he cannot do this unless he gives a maneh to each of them and then he can be sure that he has satisfied the requirements of justice. The Gemara (the later commentary) explains that he has no legal obligation to do this but a moral obligation if he wishes to ease his conscience. If, however, each of the two men claimed definitely that he was the person who was entitled to the money there would then be a legal obligation for a maneh to be paid to each of them.

If two men deposited some money with a third man, one of them depositing a *maneh* and the other two hundred *zuz*: This one says: "The two hundred *zuz* are mine" and the other one says: "The two hundred *zuz* are mine"—then he must give each one a *maneh* and the remainder should be left until Elijah comes. Rabbi José said: In that case what does the fraudulent one lose? But all the money should be left until Elijah comes.

The next case dealt with is that of two men each claiming that he had given a third man two hundred zuz to look after for him. The third man claims that he was only given three hundred zuz in all, two hundred from one of them, one hundred from the other. The point here is that the two men admit that only three hundred was deposited i.e. they deposited the amounts together but they differ on whose was the two hundred and whose the one hundred. Thus their case is not against the man they had left the money with, but rather with each other. What is to be done in such a case?

The ruling is that he must give one hundred to each of them for each is certainly entitled to this. As for the third hundred, which is in dispute, this must be left in the court "until Elijah comes." This refers to the ancient belief that before the Messiah comes Elijah will come to mankind to herald the coming of the Messiah. At that time he will settle all the unresolved issues in Jewish law. The meaning of the ruling is that since it cannot be determined which of the two is telling the truth the only course is to leave the money in the court indefinitely.

The second century Palestinian teacher, Rabbi José, disagrees with this ruling. He argues that if only the third hundred is left in the court there will be no incentive for the trickster to confess. It is better that all the money be left indefinitely in the court until the court can discover where the truth lies. If this is done, Rabbi José argues, the trickster will see that he is in danger of losing the hundred that is really his and he will confess in order to get this hundred at least.

The same applies to two vessels, one worth a _maneh_ and the other worth a thousand _zuz_. This one says: "The valuable vessel belongs to me" and the other one says: "The valuable one belongs to me"— then he must give the less valuable vessel to one of them and from the purchase price of the more valuable he must give the value of the lesser to the other and the remainder should be left until Elijah comes. Rabbi José said: In that case what does the fraudulent one lose? But the whole should be left until Elijah comes.

The next case is really the same as the previous one except that here the sale of the valuable vessel is involved and it might have been argued that this complicates the issue. But the Mishnah nonetheless identifies the two cases.

A point to be discussed (and this is, in fact, considered in the Gemara) is why not apply the rule of leaving it until Elijah comes to the case of the cloak described in the first paragraph. The answer is that in the case of the cloak, although one of the two appears to be a trickster, it is just possible that neither of them is a conscious trickster because each of them may genuinely believe that he found it first. In matters of finding something it frequently happens that mistakes of this nature are made. But in our case the trickster cannot honestly imagine that he deposited two hundred if he only deposited one hundred. On the other hand it will not do in our case to divide the money between them as in the case of the cloak. For in that case they are both holding the cloak when they come before the court and each has possession. But in our case the third hundred is held by the depositee and neither of the two has possession.

Can you think of a famous case in the Bible with affinities to the cases discussed here?

The Jerusalem Talmud

THE WORD TALMUD means "teaching," as does the other Aramaic word used for the same thing, "Gemara."

In our notes on the *Halakhic Midrashim* and the Mishnah we have noted that the Rabbis of the first two centuries were called *Tannaim,* "teachers." With the editing of the Mishnah around the year 200 of the present era the period of the *Tannaim* came to an end. From the third century onwards the scholars in Palestine and in the other great center of Jewish life, Babylon, felt it to be their main task to explain the Mishnah and to apply its teachings. The name given to these later teachers was *Amoraim* (plural of *Amora)* which means "expounders." It became axiomatic that an *Amora* never disagrees in matters of law with a *Tanna* unless he can find another *Tanna* to support him.

Gradually a mass of material from the *Amoraim* accumulated in both Palestine and Babylon. (There was a constant coming and going between Palestine and Babylon at this period so that Babylonian scholars and their views were well known and were quoted in Palestine and vice versa.) This was edited in Palestine some time around the year 400 and the whole is known as the Jerusalem Talmud or the Jerusalem Gemara. The Jerusalem Gemara in the form we have it today contains the Mishnah with a comment of the Gemara to many of its sections.

It should be pointed out that the term "Jerusalem" Talmud or Gemara, though very widely used, is, strictly speaking, incorrect. After the destruction of the Temple in the year 70 there were no schools in Jerusalem. The great Palestinian schools were in places like Tiberias, Sepphoris and Lydda. A more accurate name, frequently used, is the Palestinian Talmud or Gemara.

The Jerusalem Talmud is in Aramaic. It appears that in the Amoraic period the scholars used Aramaic as the language of instruction. The dialect of Aramaic used in the Jerusalem Talmud is Western Aramaic, while the Aramaic used in the Babylonian Talmud is Eastern Aramaic. The style of the Jerusalem Talmud is laconic and rather unfinished, perhaps because social conditions in Palestine at the time were so difficult that there was no time to give the material the kind of polish and elaboration we find in the Babylonian Talmud. It says a good deal about Jewish life in later centuries that the Babylonian Talmud became more authoritative than that of Jerusalem. Still.the Jerusalem Talmud was studied by scholars and it was the main authority on all those topics which it treated and the Babylonian Talmud did not.

CHAPTER 7

JERUSALEM TALMUD, TRACTATE BERAKHOT, CHAPTER 2:5

Concentration in prayer

The laws of balancing the duty of concentration in prayer against one's economic obligations.

MISHNAH

Craftsmen may recite the Shema **on the top of a tree or the top of a course of stones, but they are not allowed to say their prayers of petition there.**

The Shema is Israel's declaration of faith: "Hear O Israel, the Lord our God, the Lord is One." It is called the Shema after its opening word (Shema means "hear"). The point the Mishnah makes is that greater concentration is required for prayers of petition than for the recitation of the Shema. The Shema is a declaration but in prayers of petition a man's heart is engaged and if his mind is distracted he cannot think adequately of what he is saying. Consequently, it was permitted for workmen on the job to recite the Shema on the top of a tree or a course of stones. Even though full concentration is not possible there, the Rabbis felt that it was not right for them to take time off from the work for which they had been hired in order to come down. But since greater concentration is required for prayer the employer must allow them to come down so that they can say their prayers with full concentration.

GEMARA

When the Mishnah speaks of the "top of a tree" it refers to work-men, and when it speaks of the "top of a course of stones" it refers to craftsmen. Among the *Tannaim* it has been taught: They may pray their petitions at the top of an olive tree or a fig tree. From which it can be inferred that when working on other kinds of trees they must descend to pray. The employer, however, must always descend to pray. Why is it different with regard to an olive tree or a fig tree? Rabbi Abba and Rabbi Simon both explain it is because there is so much bother involved in descending from these two trees.

The Mishnah uses the term craftsmen (ummanim) and speaks of them as being at the top of a tree or the top of a course of stones. Now the term umman (singular of ummanim) really means a skilled craftsman, and such a person would not normally be engaged in the unskilled work generally associated with trees. Consequently, the Gemara interprets the Mishnah as referring to two kinds of workmen: a) the skilled craftsman (umman) on the "course of stones" i.e. engaged in skilled labor; b) the ordinary worker (poel) on the "top of a tree."

Although the Mishnah does not permit workmen to pray on the top of a tree another source is quoted in which an exception is made if the tree is an olive or a fig. However, the concession is only made for the workmen, who would otherwise waste the employer's time, but the employer himself must come down to pray even if he is working on the top of an olive or fig tree. The reason given for the ruling is that the olive and fig tree are different; because "there is so much bother" i.e. there are many branches on these trees and a good deal of time, belonging to the employer, would have to be wasted in the descent if the workmen were obliged to come down to pray. It is interesting to note how careful the Rabbis were in balancing the obligations of the workmen on the one hand to pray with concentration and on the other hand to save the employer's time.

It has also been taught among the *Tannaim:* A porter may recite the *Shema* even while carrying his burden on his shoulder but not when he is unloading it or when he is placing it there because his heart is not serene at that time. In any event he should not say his prayers of petition until he has unloaded it from his shoulder but if it only weighed four *kav* it is permitted. Rabbi Jonathan said: This only applies if it is properly balanced. What is meant by properly balanced? Two parts of it behind him and one part in front.

A porter, engaged to carry loads from place to place, is permitted to recite the Shema if the burden he carries is already on his shoulder. But he should not recite the Shema while loading or unloading because his mind is then absorbed in the task he is doing and he cannot achieve even the small amount of concentration required for the Shema. Since, as the Mishnah taught, greater concentration is required for prayer, the porter may not say his prayers of petition while the burden is on his shoulders. However, he is allowed to do so if it is only a light burden and if it is properly balanced so that he does not have to keep his mind on seeing that it does not fall. The definition of a "light" burden is given as four kav. A kav is a small measure of capacity equal to four log.

It has been taught among the *Tannaim*: **While reciting the** *Shema* **one should not wink one's eyes.**

Another source is now quoted in which it is stated that when a person recites the Shema he should keep his face immobile and should not wink to someone because this obviously interferes with his powers of concentration.

It has been taught among the *Tannaim*: **If workmen were doing work for their employer they should, while reciting Grace after meals, only recite the first benediction in full and should then include Jerusalem and the Land in one benediction which should conclude with a reference to the Land. But if they were working for the cost of their meals or if the employer ate with them they should recite all four benedictions. Rabbi Mana said: It can be inferred from this that it is forbidden to do any work while reciting Grace after meals, otherwise they could recite the full Grace and carry on working.**

Just as workmen have certain exceptions made for them with regard to the recitation of the Shema and saying their prayers, they are similarly exempt from reciting the full version of Grace after meals. A full Grace contains four benedictions. These are: 1) God is thanked for the food He has provided; 2) God is praised for giving Israel the Holy Land; 3) a prayer is offered to God to rebuild Jerusalem; 4) a final blessing of thanks. The ruling here is that the workmen should omit the fourth benediction and include the theme of the third, Jerusalem, while reciting the second benediction for the land. If the employer eats with them, however, it can be assumed that he has no objection to them reciting the full Grace. Similarly, if he does not pay them other wages but simply undertakes to provide them with meals they should recite the full Grace because this is implied in the provision of meals. From which it follows, as Rabbi Mana says, that Grace may not be recited while working otherwise they could recite the full Grace without wasting any of the employer's time.

Rabbi Samuel son of Rabbi Isaac said in the name of Rav Huna: A man should not pray while holding in his hand any kind of coin. Now this is only forbidden if the coin is in front of him but if it is behind him it is permitted. Rabbi José used to tie the coins up and hold them in his hand. What is one supposed to do with coins deposited with him by someone else? Rabbi Isaac said the verse: "And bind up the money in thy hand" (Deuteronomy 14:25) means as long as it is in thy hand. Rabbi José son of Abbun taught Rabbi Hillel, his son-in-law, to bind up money deposited with him. Rabbi Hezekiah and Rabbi Jacob son of Aha were once sitting together in a certain place and Rabbi Jacob son of Aha had some money with him. When the time came for him to say his prayers he wrapped the coins up and gave them to Rabbi Hezekiah who tied piece to piece and bound them tightly together and yet the coins slipped out. He said to him: And what of "in thy hand"?

Rav Huna was a Babylonian teacher who lived in the third century. He ruled that a man should not hold any kind of coin in his hand while saying his prayers because his mind is bound to be on the money. The Gemara comments that if the coins are behind him (perhaps attached to his waistband) there is no objection because his mind will not be on the money since he cannot see it. Rabbi José, a Palestinian of the same century, used to tie the coins in a bundle. They are then protected and he can concentrate on his prayers.

The Gemara now asks: quite apart from the question of prayer, what are considered to be adequate precautions if someone undertook to look after someone else's money? Rabbi Isaac's reply was that when such a person is carrying the money with him it is not enough for him to keep it in his pocket or even in his hand. He must tie it up so that none of it is lost. A verse is quoted in which it is stated that when money is taken from place to place the normal procedure is to tie the coins up. The Rabbi Hillel referred to here is not the famous Hillel (he is never called "Rabbi" because the title was not yet used in his day) but his great-grandson.

The text of the concluding story is not too clear. The meaning is probably that Rabbi Hezekiah contented himself with tying up the coins but he did not hold them in his hands. When they slipped out of the cloth in which they had been tied his friend said to him: "And what of 'in thy hand'?" i.e. Scripture speaks not alone of tying the coins but of holding them in the hand. If Rabbi Hezekiah had held them in his hand none would have slipped out of the cloth.

Note how two separate questions have come up in the Gemara. What began as a discussion of prayer and working ended with a discussion of proper care for funds left with you to hold. That frequently happens in both Talmuds and it is easy to see how the one discussion of holding money in prayer led to the problem of holding money for others in general.

CHAPTER 8

JERUSALEM TALMUD, TRACTATE BAVA METZIA, CHAPTER 2:5

Generosity and selfishness

The generous and ungenerous man and their motives.

*This passage deals with the theme of going beyond the strict
letter of the law. There are some things which are quite legal but
which should nevertheless be rejected by a kindly, decent human
being who wishes to show a generous spirit. In addition, such
an attitude of generosity causes others to respect the Jewish
religion. If it can inspire men to act so justly and so sympathetically
it is a noble religion. For a Jew to bring credit to his faith in
this way is called* Kiddush Ha-Shem *(the sanctification of the Name).
Hence the recurring expression: "Blessed is the God of the Jews."*

**Simeon son of Shataḥ earned his living by selling flax. His pupils
once said to him: "Rabbi! Rest a while and we will buy you a donkey
so that you will not have to work so hard." They bought him a
donkey from a certain Saracen and found that a pearl was attached
to it. When they came to him they said: "From now on you will no
longer need to toil." "Why not?" he asked. They replied: "Because
we have bought a donkey from a certain Saracen and it had a pearl
attached." He said: "Does the seller know of the pearl?" "He does
not," they replied. Whereupon he ordered them to give it back
to the seller. But did not Rav Huna Bevai son of Gozlan say in the
name of Rav: "We decided in the presence of Rabbi that even those**

authorities who rule that anything stolen from a heathen is forbidden, agree that something a heathen loses is permitted"? What think you that Simeon son of Shataḥ was a barbarian! Simeon son of Shataḥ would rather hear the heathen say: "Blessed is the God of the Jews" than have any reward this world has to offer.

Simeon son of Shataḥ was a famous Palestinian teacher who lived over two thousand years ago. The Talmud first tells the story of Simeon's behavior and then offers an objection. Like most of the other teachers of his age, you will note he made his living by engaging in business. Rav Huna Bevai said in the name of Rav (the third century Babylonian teacher) that the scholars had decided in the presence of Rabbi (the editor of the Mishnah, Rabbi Judah the Prince) that the law which requires Jews to return lost objects to their owners does not apply to heathens. Hence anything a heathen loses need not be returned to him. Since the Saracen was a heathen, although it would have been wrong to steal from him, there was no obligation for Simeon to return something the Saracen had lost through error. The reply is that even though there would have been no legal offense it was an act of great moral value to return it nonetheless. The rule about the lost property of heathens has to be understood against the background of the time when these heathens were themselves thoroughly dishonest. The law, taking this into account, refused to demand the strictest standards of honesty in dealings with them. However, this story wishes to point out that a truly honest person, faithful to religion, will not wish to avail himself of any loopholes in the law.

The name "son of Gozlan" is peculiar and can mean "son of a robber." That would be a most unlikely name so it is probable that the meaning is "son of a passage regarding robbery." Since Rav Huna Bevai was the author of this passage dealing with robbery he was called after the passage.

A similar case was that of Rabbi Ḥanina who told how some old Rabbis once bought a kor of wheat from a band of robbers and found a bundle of dinars inside it and they returned the money. Whereupon the men said: "Blessed is the God of the Jews."

A kor is a fairly large measure of wheat equal to six kav. Even though these men were themselves robbers, the "old Rabbis" did not think that this gave them the right to rob them in turn.

Abba Hosea of Traya was in charge of a laundry. Once the queen came to the laundry and lost some jewelry there. When Abba Hosea returned them to her she said: "Keep them. Of what use are they to me! I have many more and much more valuable." But he replied: "Our Law orders us to return lost property." Whereupon she said: "Blessed is the God of the Jews."

Abba Hosea similarly argues here that even if the person who has suffered the loss knows that the objects have been found and is quite willing for the finder to keep them, the finder should not do so. Rather, he should follow the spirit of Jewish law which clearly wishes that someone who has lost an object should have it returned to him.

Rabbi Samuel son of "Running-horse" went to Rome. The Empress lost a bracelet and he happened to find it. A proclamation was issued throughout the land that if anyone returns it within thirty days he will receive such-and-such a reward but if after thirty days he will lose his head. He did not return it within the thirty days but after the thirty days. She said to him: "Were you not in the province?" He replied: "Yes, I was here." She said: "But did you not hear the proclamation?" "I heard it," said he. "What did it say?" she asked. He replied: "If anyone returns it within thirty days he will receive such-and-such a reward but if he returns it after thirty days he will lose his head." She said: "In that case why did you not return it within the thirty days?" He said: "Because I did not want anyone to say that I returned it out of fear of you whereas, in fact, I returned it out of fear of the All-merciful." She said to him: "Blessed is the God of the Jews."

It might be argued here that Rabbi Samuel had no right to risk his neck simply in order to demonstrate that Judaism wishes its adherents to be honest. But we do not know the full circumstances. It may well be that in Rome at that time false accusations were being made against the Jews and Rabbi Samuel was glad of the opportunity to demonstrate the lofty standards of honesty demanded by the Jewish religion. Son of "Running-horse" is another peculiar name. It may be a nickname given to him because, as the story suggests, he was a great traveler, or it may mean that he belonged to a town of this name.

Alexander of Macedon came to visit the King of Katsia who showed him much gold and silver. Alexander said: "I am not interested in your gold and silver. I came here only to see how you conduct yourselves and how you execute justice." As they were talking a court case came before the king. A man had bought a field from his neighbor and on digging it he found a treasure buried there. The buyer claimed that he had only bought a field, not a treasure, but the seller claimed that he had sold a field and all it contained. When they had presented their arguments, the king said to one of them: "Have you a son?" "Yes," he replied. He then said to the other: "Have you a daughter?" "Yes," he replied. He said to them: "Let them get married and the treasure will belong to both of them." Alexander burst out laughing. "Why do you laugh?" asked the king. "Did I not give a right decision? How would the case have been decided in your country?" Alexander said: "We would have executed both of them and kept the treasure for ourselves." He retorted: "So much do you love gold and silver!" The king then prepared a repast for Alexander at which he offered him meat made of gold and chicken made of gold. Alexander protested: "Do you think I eat gold?" The king replied: "May that man's spirit expire! If you cannot eat it why do you love it so much?" "Does the sun shine in your country?" asked the king of Alexander. "Yes," said he. "And does the rain come down in your country?" "Yes," said he. He said: "Perhaps you have small cattle?" "Yes," said he. "May the spirit of that man expire!" said the king. "You only exist by the merit of the small cattle, as it is written: 'Man and beast Thou preservest, O Lord'" (Psalms 36:7).

Alexander of Macedon is, of course, Alexander the Great. He often is the hero of Rabbinic tales. The kingdom of Katsia was a legendary kingdom, supposedly situated on "the other side of the mountains of darkness." The unusual case was where each party to the dispute wanted nothing for himself, everything for his neighbor. The story is a critique of the policy of world conquerors who seem to be more interested in gold and gain than human happiness. The king rebuked Alexander that in a country where innocent men are executed for their gold it is only the beasts of the field who deserve to have sunshine and rain. The human beings there only enjoy these because of the merit of the animals. When man is not just he is less than the beasts.

The Babylonian Talmud

We HAVE SEEN in our note to the Jerusalem Talmud that the post-Mishnaic teachers were called *Amoraim,* "expounders," as opposed to the *Tannaim,* "the teachers." They looked upon their task as being chiefly the elucidation and application of the *Tannaitic* teachings. This activity went on for the three centuries after the editing of the Mishnah in the great Babylonian schools such as Sura and Pumbedita. Eventually all the material was collected, put into shape and, about the year 500, edited, the result being the Babylonian Talmud or Gemara. In Hebrew it is simply referred to as the *Bavli.*

Like the Jerusalem Talmud the Babylonian is in Aramaic, but in the Eastern dialect. Like the Jerusalem Talmud, too, it consists of the Mishnah with a comment on most of its sections—the Gemara. However the Babylonian Talmud treats many more parts of the Mishnah and its discussions of them are far more comprehensive than those found in the Jerusalem Talmud.

Just as the *Amoraim* considered their task to be that of elucidation (and no *Amora,* as we have seen, felt himself able to disagree with a *Tanna*) so, too, the later teachers considered the Talmud (Palestinian and Babylonian) to be the final word in Jewish law. Only rarely do we find later teachers deciding matters of law differently from the

Talmud. Once the Talmud was "closed" it became the final authority in Jewish law so that later teachers in arriving at decisions always try first to discover what light can be thrown on the subject from the Talmudic discussions.

What happens if the ruling in the Palestinian Talmud differs from that in the Babylonian (and it frequently does)? The procedure has always been to follow the Babylonian. The chief reason for this is that the schools in Palestine degenerated completely whereas Babylon became a famous center for Jews in other parts of the world. The two famous schools at Sura and Pumbedita continued with a virtually unbroken tradition right down to the eleventh century. The two heads of these schools were known as *Geonim* (singular *Gaon)* meaning "Excellencies." During the *Gaonic* period, as the post-Talmudic period was called, the heads of these two schools were in many ways the supreme authorities for Jewry in matters of Jewish law and questions would be addressed to them from many different Jewish communities. Since they were the spiritual heirs of the Babylonian *Amoraim* it was natural that they gave priority to the opinions of the Babylonian teachers. They often refer, in fact, to the Babylonian Talmud as "our" Talmud. So, to this day, when reference is made to "The" Talmud or to one of its tractates, without any further specification, it is the Babylonian Talmud which is being discussed. Citations are always given by page and side a or b.

As we noted earlier, we must not expect to find only Babylonian teachers referred to in the Babylonian Talmud. Since there were constant visits and interchanges between the two communities, the Palestinian scholars were well known in Babylon as were the Babylonian scholars in Palestine. There was, incidentally, a good deal of rivalry between the two communities. The Palestinians considered themselves to be the better scholars. In one ironic passage a Palestinian scholar says that the reason the Babylonian scholars look like angels (i.e. in the splendor of their dress) is because they are insufficiently learned to impress people with their knowledge, so they have to impress with their dress. Some Babylonian scholars did, in fact, emigrate to Palestine, believing that they would learn far more there. But it was a two-way traffic. Eventually Babylon became the more important center because Palestine at this period did not provide comfortable surroundings for study whereas the Persian rulers of Babylon were, on the whole, favorably disposed toward the Jews and gave them ample opportunities for living a life in which scholars find the leisure to study.

CHAPTER 9

Conditions of employment

The laws of explicit statements when workmen are engaged.

MISHNAH

If a man hired laborers and ordered them to work early in the morning and late at night he cannot compel them to work early and late if it is not the custom to do so in that place.

In the time of the Mishnah it was usual for laborers on farms (which is what is meant in the case under discussion) to work from sunrise to sunset with breaks for meals. The law was that any conditions on such matters as hours of work could be drawn up between employer and laborers at the time of contracting, but what if no explicit conditions were drawn up? Then, the Mishnah states, the local custom in these matters should be followed because it is proper to assume that, in the absence of an explicit stipulation, both sides intended the contract to be in accordance with that custom. Consequently the Mishnah rules that if suddenly the employer demanded that the laborers work overtime, by coming into work while it is still dark and by leaving after sunset, they can refuse to do this and the employer cannot withhold their wages on the grounds that they have not honored their contract. Since the local custom in that place is that workers do not work overtime, an explicit undertaking is required otherwise the employer has no case.

In a place in which it is the custom for the employer to provide them with meals he must do so. In a place in which it is the custom for him to provide them with sweetmeats he must do so. Local custom is always binding in these matters.

Similarly, rules the Mishnah, with regard to the employer's contract to provide his workers with meals. If the local custom is that an employer does provide the meals the workers can demand that he do this for them even though there had been no explicit contract that he do it. The undertaking is implicit in the local custom which both parties are assumed to have followed unless there had been an express condition to the contrary. And this applies, too, says the Mishnah, if the local custom is that the employer provide his workers not alone with plain meals but with delicacies of various kinds, "sweetmeats."

It once happened that Rabbi Johanan son of Matteya said to his son: Go and hire some laborers to work for us. The son went and hired them and undertook to provide them with food. When the son came and told his father what he had done the father said: My son, now even if you will provide them with the kind of feast that Solomon prepared in his time you have not fulfilled your obligations to them since they are the sons of Abraham, Isaac and Jacob. Go and say to them before they begin to work: I engage you on the understanding that you have no claim on me except to provide you with bread and pulse. But Rabbi Simeon son of Gamaliel said that there was no need for him to have made this stipulation since local custom is always binding in these matters.

The Mishnah then records an actual case. Rabbi Johanan son of Matteya lived in the second century. He was evidently a farmer of some substance. Naturally any contract undertaken by the son of the house with the approval of his father is binding.
The son when engaging the workmen undertook explicitly to provide them with meals. The question here is what can legitimately be covered by the term "meals"? Supposing the workmen turned up their noses at the meals provided and said: Do you call this a meal? We want a fine repast. Can they legitimately demand this? Rabbi Johanan held that his son had, in fact, committed him to whatever the workers would demand in the way of meals. Even if

he provided them with the kind of meal prepared by King Solomon for the people it would still be insufficient if the workers objected since, although they were ordinary workmen, they were the descendants of Abraham, Isaac and Jacob and were entitled to be treated as princes. The only thing to do was for the son to make it clear to them before they started work (once they had started the contract had come into operation and would have to be honored) that the contract did not include the provision of elaborate meals but only bread and pulse. Pulse means things like beans and peas, evidently eaten with bread in those days.

When Rabban Gamaliel heard of this he remarked that Rabbi Johanan need not have been so concerned that the workers would make excessive demands for, he argued, local custom is to be followed and they could only ask for that to which local custom entitled them.

GEMARA

Is it not obvious? The case in question is where the employer gave them a higher wage than was normal. Here it might have been argued that the employer could say: The reason I gave you a higher wage than is normal is so that you will work early in the morning and late at night. So the law tells us that the laborers can reply: The reason that you gave us a higher wage than is normal is that we should do a better job than is normal.

The Gemara asks a question concerning the first rule of the Mishnah that if the local custom is not for them to work early and late the employer cannot demand it. Is this not obvious, asks the Gemara. Since local custom is not to work early and late how can the employer possibly demand this? If he intended to contract for early and late work he should have stipulated this at the time when he engaged the workmen. To this the Gemara replies that we are dealing with a case where the employer had undertaken to provide the workmen with higher wages than normal in that district. Here it might have been argued that the higher wage in itself implies a contract to work longer hours than normal, otherwise why should the workers imagine that the employer would give them higher than normal wages. But the Mishnah still rules that the employer has no case because the workmen can argue *that they were under the impression that the higher wage was for better quality work.*

Resh Lakish said: A laborer must return home from work in his own time but can leave to go to work in his employer's time, as it is said: "The sun ariseth, they gather themselves together, and lay them down in their dens. Man goeth forth unto his work and to his labor until the evening" (Psalms 104:22,23). But why not see what the local custom is in this matter? It is a new town (where a local custom has not yet been established). But why not see what the local custom is in the place from which they came? They came from many different places (with differing local customs). Or if you want I can say that the case dealt with here is where the employer says to them: I hire you in the manner of the workmen as mentioned in the Torah.

Resh Lakish lived in Palestine in the third century. His full name is Rabbi Simeon of Lakish. We have seen that farm work was generally undertaken from sunrise to sunset. Does this mean that the worker must leave home before sunrise to be ready for work at sunrise and that he must work until sunset and then make his way home? Resh Lakish argues that since Scripture states that a man goes out to work at sunrise and works until the evening it would seem that Scripture has in mind as normal procedure that a worker need not set out before sunrise (hence he sets out in his employer's time) but must stay at work until sunset. Thus the workers are paid from sunrise to sunset, but this includes the time in the morning that it takes the worker to reach the farm.
 Now the Gemara, relying on the rule of the Mishnah, objects that surely it all depends on the local custom. For Scripture is not laying down a law but simply stating casually that men in those days generally worked according to these conditions. But there is no suggestion that these conditions must always be binding upon employers and workmen. Indeed, the Mishnah has clearly ruled that if local custom is as Resh Lakish says, there is no need for his rule and if, on the other hand, local custom differs from his rule his rule would, in fact, have to be set aside. The reply is that normally, indeed, it is local custom which determines conditions but Resh Lakish deals with a new town in which there is no local custom in these matters. But still, objects the Gemara, the workers must have come from somewhere and it can be

assumed that the local custom of the place from which they come would be followed. To this the reply is given that we are dealing with a case where the workers came from many different places, each with its own custom. Consequently local custom cannot here be followed and here the law would follow Resh Lakish.

Finally, the Gemara states that, indeed, in normal cases it is local custom which decides in these matters. But Resh Lakish deals with a case in which the employer expressly stated that he did not wish to follow the local custom but wished to follow the practice of Biblical times. If the workers agree to this all that is then required is to determine what was the practice in Biblical times, and it is of this which Resh Lakish informs us. It is incidentally interesting that the Gemara refers to the Torah although, in fact, the verse quoted by Resh Lakish is in the book of Psalms. Generally speaking, in the Rabbinic literature the word Torah refers to the Five Books of Moses but sometimes, as here, it has the wider meaning of the whole Bible.

CHAPTER 10

Cheating in buying and selling

Legitimate and illegitimate ways of attracting business.

MISHNAH

Rabbi Judah says: A shopkeeper must not give the children (who are sent by their mothers to do the shopping) burnt ears of corn and nuts because this encourages them to come to his shop (and it is unfair to the other shopkeepers). But the Sages permit it. Nor should a shopkeeper sell below the market price. But the Sages say: Good for him. A shopkeeper, says Abba Saul, should not sift crushed beans. But the Sages permit it. But they agree that he should not sift them only at the top of the container for this would amount to nothing else than deceit. It is forbidden to paint (so as to improve their appearance) human beings (sold as slaves) or animals or vessels (before selling them).

Rabbi Judah lived in Palestine in the second century. He was of the opinion that a shopkeeper should not give small gifts to the young children who are sent to buy goods in his shop because in so doing he is taking unfair advantage of other shopkeepers. Whenever the children are sent to buy something they will prefer to buy at his shop in expectation of the nuts and burnt ears of corn they will be given. Burnt ears of corn were, in those days, tasty titbits like candy nowadays. The Sages, the other Rabbis of Rabbi Judah's day, do, however, permit it for the reason mentioned in the Gemara. There is nothing to prevent the other shopkeepers doing likewise or even going one better. If Rabbi Judah were alive today he would no doubt object to the practice of some firms of giving gift vouchers and so forth with the goods they sell in order to increase sales, but the Sages would evidently see no objection to this. Rabbi Judah seems to be concerned with the protection of other shopkeepers but the Sages are more concerned with the benefits to the general public.

The Mishnah goes on to say that in the opinion of some teachers it is forbidden for a shopkeeper to sell his goods below the market price. This is also considered to be unfair to other shopkeepers. But here again the Sages permit it. They would, indeed, encourage this kind of competition because it helps to bring prices down and benefits the customers. In our society these matters are often regulated by the government and, of course, Jewish law would see no objection to price controls.

Abba Saul lived in Palestine in the second century. He forbids a shopkeeper to sift crushed beans. Crushed beans were a usual food in Palestine at this period. Sifting the beans means removing some bad ones so that all the beans look good to eat. Abba Saul is of the opinion that this may make the goods look so appetizing that the shopkeeper will be tempted to raise the price. But the Sages permit it since the shopkeeper does not engage in any deceit. He does not pull wool over the customers' eyes. If, however, the shopkeeper only sifts the beans at the top of the large container from which he sells them, all agree that it is forbidden. For in this case the customer sees only the good beans and imagines that he is buying these whereas the shopkeeper may dig down into the container when measuring out the beans and mix bad with the good.

The Mishnah concludes with further examples of cheating. It is forbidden to paint, so as to make them attractive, human beings, animals and vessels. The reference to human beings is to slaves. At that time slavery was not outlawed although Jewish teachers did all they could to make Jewish slave-owners treat their slaves well. Nowadays one can think of many examples of the kind of sharp practice forbidden here. Some of these are: faking paintings so that they appear to be the work of the great masters; faking more recent objects to make them look like genuine antiques; forging documents; tampering with the mileage gauge of a car to *suggest that the mileage is less than it really is; pretending that goods are offered at sale price when, in fact, there has been no reduction.*

GEMARA

What is the reason of the Rabbis? Because the shopkeeper can say to his competitors: I give them nuts; you can give them plums.

The debate between Rabbi Judah and the Sages is explained as above.

"Nor should a shopkeeper sell below the market price. But the Sages say: Good for him." What is the reason of the Rabbis? Because he helps to make the price more flexible.

The second debate is explained as above. The Sages argue that when shopkeepers lower the price and there is keen competition, prices will come down to the benefit of the customers.

"A shopkeeper, says Abba Saul, should not sift crushed beans. But the Sages permit it." Who are these Sages? Rabbi Aha. For it has been taught: Rabbi Aha permits it with regard to goods that can be seen.

The Sages of the Mishnah are identified with Rabbi Aha (the plural "Sages" will then be used rather loosely). Rabbi Aha, too, lived in Palestine in the second century. His argument is that since the customer can see the goods i.e. he can see that the bad beans have been removed, there is no deceit on the part of the shopkeeper.

"It is forbidden to paint—" Our Rabbis taught: An animal (for sale) should not be made to look stiff; the insides of an animal should not be blown up; and meat should not be soaked in water. What is meant by "An animal should not be made to look stiff"? Here (in Babylon) they understand it to mean that the animal should not be fed with bran-broth. Zeiri said in Rav Kahana's name: It means that the animal's hair should not be brushed up.

Three further examples are now given of cheating in a sale. The hair of an animal up for sale should not be made stiffer than it really is so that the buyers might imagine that the animal is plump and well-conditioned. When intestines are sold in a butcher shop the butcher should not inflate them artificially to make them look larger than they really are (the reference appears to be when they are sold by size; if they are sold by weight it would not make any difference). Lean meat on sale should not be soaked in water to make it look fat. The Gemara explains the first case in two ways. In Babylon this was explained to mean that the animal is fed with a soup or broth made from bran which has the effect of making the animal's hair stand on end. The other explanation is that the hair of the animal is combed with a stiff brush to make it stand on end.

Samuel permitted fringes to be added to a cloak. Rav Judah permitted fine cloths to be rubbed and polished. Rabbah permitted cloth made of hemp to be beaten. Rava permitted arrows to be painted. Rav Pappa son of Samuel permitted baskets to be painted. But do we not learn in the Mishnah that it is forbidden to paint vessels? There is no contradiction. The Mishnah refers to old goods while these Rabbis refer to new goods.

Samuel lived in Babylon in the third century. Rav Judah (not to be confused with the Palestinian teacher Rabbi Judah mentioned in the Mishnah) was Samuel's pupil. Rabbah was a Babylonian teacher of the generation after Rav Judah and Rava was Rabbah's pupil. Rav Pappa son of Samuel was a contemporary of Rava. Samuel argues that the rule of the Mishnah against "painting" vessels would not apply to fringes added to a garment to make it more attractive since the garment itself is not touched up. To take a modern example there would obviously be no objection to a shopkeeper presenting his goods in attractive wrappings. Similarly Rav Judah sees no objection to the polishing of fine cloths to bring out the gloss and Rabbah no objection to making the best of cloth of hemp that is to be sold. Rava and Rav Pappa permitted arrows and baskets to be painted. This does seem to contradict the ruling of the Mishnah and the Gemara. But a distinction is drawn between old and new vessels. There is no objection to making arrows, baskets (or anything else) more attractive by painting if the goods are new. The Mishnah only objects to a shopkeeper camouflaging old goods by painting them so that they appear to be new and the customer is thereby misled.

What is meant by painting men? As in the case of a certain elderly slave who dyed his hair and beard and came to Raba and asked him to buy him as a slave. Raba quoted: "Let the poor be members of thy household." When he came to Rav Pappa son of Samuel he bought him. One day Rav Pappa ordered the slave to bring him some water to drink whereupon the slave washed his hair and beard white again and said: Look I am older than your father. Rav Pappa quoted against himself the verse: "The righteous is delivered out of trouble and another cometh in his stead" (Proverbs 11:8).

An example is given of how slaves would dye their hair and beard in order to appear younger than they really were. The fact that the heroes of this tale are Rava and Rav Pappa son of Samuel, mentioned above, may be no more than a coincidence. But it is also possible that the slave tried to sell himself to these two teachers because they were known to have permitted painting of a kind, as above, and the slave might have thought that he would succeed with them. Or perhaps the two teachers were moved by their experience with the slave to study and pronounce on the laws of deceit in buying and selling! Rava quotes from an earlier source (actually from the section of the Mishnah known as "Ethics of the Fathers"): "Let the poor be members of thy household." He understood this to mean that a man able to afford servants should engage poor people for the work rather than buy slaves. Rav Pappa did buy the slave. It is interesting that when the slave pointed out to Rav Pappa that he was old the Rabbi did not compel him to work, as the law permitted him to do. He evidently believed that it was wrong to treat a slave as less than a human being and force him to work. Rav Pappa uses the verse to say that Raba, being righteous, was spared the trouble with the slave while he, Rav Pappa, was not. The verse quoted by Rav Pappa actually speaks of the "wicked" taking the place of the righteous, but since he applied the verse to himself he naturally preferred to soften the blow by substituting the word "another" for the "wicked."

CHAPTER 11

BABYLONIAN TALMUD, TRACTATE BAVA METZIA, PAGES 59a–b; 86a

The scope of human reasoning

Human beings decide what it is that
God would have them do.

We have been taught: "If an oven was cut up into sections and sand put between each section, Rabbi Eliezer argues that such an oven can never become unclean but the Sages argue that it can. Such was the oven of *Akhnai*." What is meant by *Akhnai*? Rav Judah said in the name of Samuel: The meaning is that the Sages surrounded it with arguments like this snake and they declared it unclean. We have been taught: On that day Rabbi Eliezer replied with every argument in the world and yet the Sages refused to budge. He then said: If my decision is right this carob-tree will prove it, and the carob-tree then moved a distance of one hundred cubits. Others say that it moved four hundred cubits. The Sages replied: No proof can be brought from a carob-tree. He then said: If my decision is right the stream of water will prove it, and the stream of water then moved backwards. But the Sages replied: No proof can be brought from a stream of water. He then said: If my decision is right the walls of the House of Study will prove it, and the walls of the House of Study began to cave in. Rabbi Joshua shouted at the walls: If scholars are in disagreement about a decision in Jewish law what business is it of yours! The result was that the walls did not cave in entirely, out of respect for Rabbi Joshua, but neither did they return to their previous upright position, out of respect for Rabbi Eliezer, and thus they still stand in an inclined position. He then said to them: If my decision is right let it be proved from Heaven. A voice came from Heaven saying: What do you want of Rabbi Eliezer? The ruling is always in accordance with his views. Rabbi Joshua arose to his feet at this point and said: "It is not in heaven" (Deuteronomy 30:12). What did Rabbi Joshua mean? Rabbi Jeremiah said: What he meant to say was that no notice should be taken of a voice from Heaven in matters of Jewish law once the Torah has been given on Sinai. For Thou hast written in Thy Torah: "After the majority must one incline" (Exodus 23:2). Rabbi Nathan met Elijah and asked him: What did the Holy one, blessed be He, do at that time? Elijah replied: He laughed with joy saying: My sons have gotten the better of Me, My sons have gotten the better of Me.

Obviously this story and the next have legendary elements but they are a remarkable affirmation of the role of human reasoning in matters of Jewish law. Rabbi Eliezer and Rabbi Joshua both lived in the first half of the second century. Rabbi Eliezer (also known as Rabbi Eliezer the Great) is renowned in the Talmudic literature as the man who sticks to his views through thick and thin and refuses to give them up since he believes they are true. Rav Judah is the third century Babylonian teacher and pupil of Samuel whose views he quotes here and very frequently. Rabbi Jeremiah is a fourth century Palestinian teacher. Finally, Rabbi Nathan is a second century Palestinian teacher. We shall now explain point by point.

The actual debate between Rabbi Eliezer and the Sages is recorded in the Mishnah in another tractate, hence the quote is introduced by the words "We have been taught." The question is this. According to the laws of purity and impurity in Temple times, as found in the book of Leviticus, a vessel which comes into contact with a corpse, a dead reptile and the like becomes "unclean" and no sacred food (e.g. the tithe given to the priest) may be cooked in it. But the rule is that only a vessel or something like one can become unclean. Consequently, although an ordinary oven can also become unclean, it can be argued that a sectional oven with only sand connecting the sections is not considered to be like a vessel and therefore can never be unclean. This is in fact Rabbi Eliezer's argument. But the Sages are of the opinion that since the sand makes it fit for use as an oven it is to be treated like any other oven and it can become unclean. The Mishnah concludes that this was the oven of Akhnai.

Now the word Akhnai may have been the name of an oven-maker or the name of the owner of the oven. But Rav Judah in the name of Samuel puns on the word which can also mean a snake. Hence the explanation is given that it was called the "snake oven" because just as a snake coils itself into a circle the Sages surrounded the oven with arguments, that is to say they produced argument after argument in order to show that their conclusions were correct.

Another source is then quoted. This is a Baraita, a source outside the Mishnah but dating from the same period (probably late second century). Here it is said that at first Rabbi Eliezer tried to produce arguments to show he was right but when he failed to convince his colleagues he resorted to miracles. A carob-tree is a tree which grows in Palestine, having a bean-like fruit. When the tree miraculously moved, Rabbi Eliezer thought that this would confirm the argument, but he did not reckon with the toughness of the Sages. The Sages refused to budge even in the teeth of this miracle and that of the stream of water flowing backwards. There is a touch of humor in the account of the battle of the walls, "and thus they still stand . . ."

Then comes the "punch-line" of the story. Observing that ordinary miracles are insufficient to convince his colleagues, Rabbi Eliezer appeals to Heaven. God responds and a voice comes from Heaven to declare that Rabbi Eliezer is right. One would have thought that this would confirm the argument even for the most skeptical but Rabbi Joshua (one of the Sages) still refuses to budge. He simply quotes the verse in Deuteronomy: "It is not in Heaven." Rabbi Jeremiah explains that Rabbi Joshua meant to say that the Torah was given by God but once it has been given to human beings it is they and not God who must decide which view is correct.

It is to be noted that the story does not suggest that Rabbi Joshua is questioning whether the voice from Heaven is authentic, whether it is the voice of God. What the story says is that God cannot contradict Himself and once He has given the Torah, in which it is stated that in matters of dispute the majority view is followed, He cannot intervene on the side of the minority. What this probably means is something like this. When a matter of law has to be decided, the only reasonable way is to be democratic and follow the majority of scholars. This is not because we can guarantee that the majority is always right. It may frequently be wrong. But if anarchy is to be avoided the majority must be followed right or wrong. Hence God's voice in our story did not speak falsely. God declares that from the absolute point of view Rabbi Eliezer's opinion was the right one but it is not with absolute truth that human judges and scholars are concerned but with the truth as a guide for life and as applied by humans. All this is a very subtle subject. It can serve as a useful topic for a general discussion.

The story concludes with the account of how Elijah the prophet, who did not die and was believed to appear at times to chosen Rabbis, appeared to Rabbi Nathan. When Rabbi Nathan asked Elijah what God's reaction, as it were, was to the bold saying of Rabbi Joshua, Elijah replied that God was glad that His sons had gotten the better of Him. The meaning here is that God wants man to stand on his own feet and God is very pleased when this happens even in the bold manner of a Rabbi Joshua.

[Rabbah bar Nahmani had to flee for his life and] he sat upon the trunk of a palmtree and studied. At that time there was a debate going on in the Heavenly College between the Holy One, blessed be He, and the members of the College concerning possible cases of plague-spots. If the bright spot was first and then the white hair, he is unclean. If the white hair is first and then the bright spot, he is clean. If there is a doubt as to which is first: The Holy One, blessed be He, said that in this case he is clean but all the members of the College said that in this case he is unclean. Who shall decide which view is correct? said they. Let Rabbah bar Nahmani decide, for Rabbah bar Nahmani always says: I am the outstanding authority on the laws of plagues and tents. They sent a messenger for him but the Angel of Death was unable to get near because he did not pause in his studies even for a moment. In the meantime the wind began to blow and when he heard the rustling in the bushes he thought it was a troop of soldiers. He prayed: Let that man die rather than be handed over to the government. As he was dying he said: Clean, clean. A voice then came from Heaven saying: Happy are you, O Rabbah bar Nahmani. Your body is pure and your soul has departed in Purity!

Another story from the same tractate of the Talmud with more
or less the same theme, concerns the supremacy of human reasoning
in deciding Jewish law. Rabbah bar Naḥmani was born around the
year 270. He was the foremost scholar in Babylon in his day.
The story begins by telling how Rabbah was obliged to fly for his
life because informers had unjustly accused him of causing
thousands of his pupils to evade paying their taxes.

In the book of Leviticus, chapter 13, verses 1-13, we read that
if a man has a plague spot on his skin and it is bright and he has
a white hair in the spot he is unclean (and must stay outside
the camp until he is clean again). Now since Scripture speaks of
"a white hair in the bright spot" the Rabbis argue that he is only
unclean if the order is first the bright spot and then the white
hair, not the other way round. But supposing there was a doubt
which of the two had been first? Here God ruled that he is
clean, but all the members of the Heavenly College ruled that he
is unclean. The members of the Heavenly College are the dead
scholars who still study the Torah in Heaven. Note that here, too,
the members of the College have a right to disagree with God.
However, they too are no longer on earth and hence the real
decision has to be made by a human authority. Rabbah is asked for
his decision.

Rabbah evidently prided himself on being the outstanding
authority on plagues (i.e. the laws of plague-spots) and tents (the
laws regarding a corpse in a tent). These laws were considered to
be particularly knotty. If the Rabbis wished to say of a man
that he was a great legal scholar they would speak of him as an
authority on plagues and tents. The Rabbis believed that since the
Torah is called the Torah of life it was impossible for the Angel
of Death to take away the soul of a man while he was studying the
Torah. The term "that man" in the story is, of course, Rabbah
himself. It was the idiom in Rabbinic times for a person when
referring to something unpleasant happening to himself to speak
of it as if it were happening to another—"that man." Note what
the Rabbis considered a desirable end, expiring in the purity of
devotion to Torah.

Parents and children

*The laws of children honoring and respecting
their parents.*

Our Rabbis taught: How are we to understand *respect* **for parents and**
honor **of parents?** *Respect* **means that a son should not stand or sit
in his father's place, that he should not contradict his father's
opinions and that when his father argues with another person he
should not take it upon himself to decide which of them is right.**
Honor **means that a son should provide his father with food and
drink, with clothes and garments, and should assist him as he enters
and leaves a room.**

*The approximate date of this section (compiled in Palestine) is the
second century. A passage introduced in the Talmud with the
words: "Our Rabbis taught" is known as a Baraita ("outside teaching"
i.e. an authoritative teaching but not included in the Mishnah,
edited around the year 200). There are two Scriptural verses
concerning the attitude of children to parents. These are: 1) "Honor
thy father and thy mother" (Exodus 20:12). 2) "Ye shall respect thy
mother and father" (Leviticus 19:3). According to Jewish teaching
the verses refer to two separate duties,.honoring parents and
respecting them. Hence the Baraita seeks to define what duties
are covered by respect and what by honor. The definition is given
in terms of concrete examples as if to say, that is what a son must do*

if he wishes to obey the rules regarding respect and honor.
Although the Baraita speaks of a son and his father it is, of
course, obvious that what is meant is the relationship of a son
or daughter to father or mother. Some of the later commentators
to the Talmud note that there is no reference here to a duty
of obeying parents and they therefore draw the conclusion that
Judaism does not demand that a child obey his parents where
there is good reason for disobedience. If, for example, parents
order a son or daughter to give up the girl or boy they had chosen
to marry there is no obligation for the child to bow to the
parent's wishes.

Three examples are given to illustrate what respect means: 1) The
son should not stand or sit in his father's place. 2) The son
should not contradict his father's opinions. 3) When the father
is involved in a controversy with another the son should not decide
which of them is right. Some of the commentators understand
1) literally. If the father has a special chair in the home or seat
in the Synagogue the son, out of respect, should not occupy his
father's place. Others understand it figuratively. The son should not
occupy any of his father's social positions without his consent
i.e. take his place as chairman of a society or director of a company.
Some of the commentators understand 2) to mean that the son
should never contradict his father's opinion but he may argue
respectfully for his own opinions if these are at variance with
those of his father. 3) means that the son should not decide even
in favor of his father for by so doing he implies that he is
worthy to be a judge of his father's opinions.

Three examples are given to illustrate what honor means:
1) Providing the parent with food and drink. 2) Providing the parent
with clothes. 3) Escorting a parent in and out of a room. In our
society this latter would include such courtesies as opening doors
for parents. 1) and 2) can either mean that the son is obliged to buy
his father food, drink and clothes or that the son is merely to
serve his father at table and help him to dress himself i.e. serve
as his valet. This is the point of discussion in 2—whether the son
or the father is obliged to pay for the means of honor. The
expression "clothes and garments" is somewhat odd and in some
texts the reading is, instead, "clothes and shoes" which is less
strange since in Rabbinic times shoes were sufficiently costly to be
treated as a separate item.

The Rabbis asked: Who has to pay for the food, drink and clothes by which a son honors his father? Rav Judah said: The son. Rav Nathan son of Oshia said: The father. The Rabbis instructed Rabbi Jeremiah (others say it was the son of Rabbi Jeremiah) to follow the opinion of the teacher who said: The father.

Rav Judah and Rav Nathan son of Oshia lived in Babylon in the first half of the third century. As we have seen, their debate concerns the correct interpretation of the Baraita. Is a son obliged to buy his parents food, drink and clothes and/or is he only obliged to serve up the food and so forth? According to Rav Judah, honoring parents means that the son is obliged to buy these things for his parents (unless, of course, they do not wish him to do so). According to Rav Nathan there is no such obligation. Keep these two men and their views in mind as most of the rest of the passage argues one against the other. The passage states that the later Rabbis decided that Rav Nathan was right and they instructed Rabbi Jeremiah accordingly. Rabbi Jeremiah lived in the fourth century. He was born and educated in Babylon but, thinking more of Jewish scholarship in Palestine, went there to continue his studies.

Most of the post-Talmudic teachers follow this ruling and state that a father cannot, in the name of the duty of honoring parents, demand that his son provide him with his life's needs. However, they go on to say, this does not apply where the father is too poor to afford to buy these things for himself. Obviously Judaism does not teach that a rich son may avoid his responsibilities to his parents and leave them to be supported by charity.

An objection was raised: It is said: "Honor thy father and thy mother" (Exodus 20:12) and it is said "Honor the Lord with thy substance" (Proverbs 3:9). Just as monetary expense is involved in the second case, so too monetary expense may be involved in the first case. But if you say that the father pays for the honor the son gives him how is the son involved in monetary expense? He loses the value of the time he spends.

An attempt is now made to prove from an earlier source whether Rav Judah or Rav Nathan is right. Another Baraita is quoted (also dating from approximately second-century Palestine). Here it is stated that the duty of honor is owed both to God and to parents and a Scriptural verse is quoted for each. Now, the argument runs, since the two are compared in Scripture it follows that whatever is true of one must be true of the other and since the duty of honoring God involves what the Gemara calls "loss of pocket" (i.e. monetary expense for a Synagogue and its equipment or other religious requirements) honoring parents is a duty which must be performed even when it involves "loss of pocket." This would seem to support Rabbi Judah who, indeed, demands that the son pay for his father's needs. But if one follows Rabbi Nathan, who rules that the son is only obliged to serve his father at table and the like, how can he be considered "out of pocket" through honoring parents? The answer given is that the son could have used the time he spends in honoring his parents in gainful employment so that, indirectly at least, the duty of honoring parents can involve the son in loss of pocket.

Come and hear: "Two brothers or two partners or a father and a son or a teacher and pupil may redeem the second tithe one for the other and may give to one another the poor man's tithe." But if you say that the son has to pay for the honor he gives his father it would mean that he pays his debt with money belonging to the poor. The reference here is to extra luxuries. But if this is so why do we read further: "Rabbi Judah said: Cursed be one who gives his father poor man's tithe." If it is only a matter of extra luxuries why should he not do so? Even so it is unworthy.

Another attempt is now made to prove which view is the right one. The attempted proof is from still another Baraita. The words introducing it are "Come and hear," the usual Talmudic formula for introducing a proof of this kind.

In early Talmudic times there was an elaborate system of tithing by which the farmer gave of his produce. The first tenth (tithe) of the farmer's corn, wine and oil, for example, was called the first tithe and had to be given to the Levite who had no land of his own. The "second tithe" was not given away to others but it had to be taken to Jerusalem, the holy city, to be consumed there when the farmer went there on pilgrimage. But if the farmer wished to do so he could "redeem" the produce involved in this second tithe and simply set aside its value in money. This money would then become sacred, like the original tithe, and would have to be spent in Jerusalem, but in that case the original food and drink would return to the ordinary status. However, if the farmer himself put up the money in place of the produce he would be obliged to add an extra fifth to its cost. If it were redeemed by someone else, who wanted to buy it, the latter would only be obliged to give the actual cost.

Once in three years, however, the second tithe became the "poorman's tithe"; that is to say, it was set aside to be given to the poor. Even a poor man who had some poorman's tithe from his own small field could not keep it for himself but was obliged to give it to another poor man. These laws set the problem.

It follows from what has been said that a man cannot redeem his own second tithe (unless he is prepared to add an extra fifth) and he cannot keep for himself the poorman's tithe. The question discussed in the Baraita is whether someone very close to a person is treated as the person himself with regard to these rules. The Baraita rules that no matter how close are the ties between two persons they are to be treated as strangers for this purpose. Hence the Baraita states that two brothers (who live off the family estate), or two partners (sharing the produce of a farm), or a father and son or a teacher and pupil may redeem (without the extra fifth) one another's second tithe and give to one another (if they are poor) their poorman's tithe.

From all this it clearly emerges that a son may give his father poorman's tithe if the father is poor—and now we are back to the original problem. If the son has an obligation to pay for his father's needs, as Rav Judah teaches, then by giving the father the poorman's tithe the son is, in fact, using this tithe to pay his debts. Consequently he is using this tithe for his own obligations which is forbidden. The answer is that the Baraita does not intend to permit giving the poorman's tithe to pay for the father's actual living needs but only for the purpose of providing him with luxuries. Since the son has no obligation, even according to Rav Judah, to provide his father with luxuries his doing so with his poorman's tithe cannot be considered as if he were paying his own debts.

But an objection is then raised. In the same Baraita it is said that Rabbi Judah (an earlier second century Palestinian teacher, hence given the title Rabbi, and not to be confused with the Babylonian teacher Rav Judah one of the two people engaged in our debate) disagrees with the view that a son may give his father poorman's tithe. But if we are only dealing with provision of extra luxuries

*why should Rabbi Judah object? To this the reply is given that
nonetheless Rabbi Judah feels it to be disgraceful for a son to give
his father poorman's tithe even though the purpose is only
to provide the father with extra luxuries. Rabbi Judah holds that
these, too, should be provided out of the son's own pocket.*

**Come and hear: They asked Rabbi Eliezer: "To what extent should
honoring parents go?" He replied: "To the extent that even if the
father takes a bag of money and throws it into the sea in his son's
presence the son should not insult him." But if the duty of honoring
parents is paid for by the father it is the father's money that he throws
into the sea and what difference does this make to the son? It is the
son's inheritance that he throws away.**

*Another Baraita is now quoted. Here Rabbi Eliezer (second
century, Palestine) answers, in reply to a question his pupils put
to him, that the duty of honoring parents demands that a son
should offer no protest even if his father throws away a bag of money.
According to Rav Judah's view that the son pays for his father's
needs, this prohibition would make sense. Rabbi Eliezer will be
speaking of a father who throws his son's money away. If it is
according to Rav Nathan's view the son has a right to protest if
the father throws the son's money away (since there is no
obligation for a son to suffer loss of pocket in honoring his parents).
Consequently, Rabbi Eliezer's statement must be understood
also as speaking of the case where the father throws his own money
away. If this is so it is hard to see why the son should be upset. He
is not obligated to replace it. To this the reply is given that the
son knows that one day he will inherit his father's wealth. Although
at the moment it is the father's money it would have been
inherited by the son if the father had not thrown it away.
Consequently, the son would feel bound to protest, yet he refrains
from doing so in honor of his father.*

**As in the case of Rabbah son of Rav Huna: Rav Huna tore some
silks in the presence of his son Rabbah, saying to himself: "Let us see
if he will lose his temper." But how could Rav Huna do this? Rabbah
might have lost his temper and then Rav Huna would have offended
against the law: "Thou shalt not put a stumbling block before a
blind man" (Leviticus 19:14). Rav Huna waived his rights. But Rav
Huna offended against the law which says that it is forbidden to**

destroy anything of value. He tore it at the seams. This, then, might have been the reason for Rabbah not losing his temper. Rav Huna did it on an occasion when Rabbah was already in a temper.

An actual case is now quoted. Rav Huna (a Babylonian teacher of the third century) tore up some costly silks in the presence of his son, Rabbah, as a test; that is to say he wished to know whether Rabbah would be strong enough to exercise self-control and still show respect for his father.

An objection is raised to Rav Huna's test. The Biblical prohibition of placing a stumbling block in front of a blind man includes the prohibition of causing another to sin. Now if Rabbah had lost his temper and insulted his father he would have committed a sin and for this Rav Huna would have been ultimately responsible. How, then, could Rav Huna have acted in this way? The reply is given that Rav Huna waived his rights as a father and therefore even if Rabbah had lost his temper no sin would have resulted since there is no obligation to honor parents when the parents expressly waive their parental rights.

A further objection is then raised to Rav Huna's test. It is a principle of Rabbinic law that it is forbidden to destroy anything of value. How, then, could Rav Huna have destroyed costly silks? The answer is that he only tore the silks at the seams and since they could be sewn together again there was no permanent damage. But in that case, it is objected, the test fails, since Rabbah may not have lost his temper simply because he saw that his father was not really destroying anything of value. To this the reply is given that Rav Huna carried out the test at a moment when Rabbah was already in a rage and it must therefore have been very tempting to him to insult his father even though no permanent damage was done to the silks.

In other parts of the Talmud the following further examples are given of the prohibition of placing a stumbling block before the blind. If a Nazirite (who has taken a vow not to drink wine) asks you for a glass of wine you are not to give it to him if otherwise he could not have obtained it. If someone asks you for advice you must not give him advice that will be harmful to him.

This passage is an excellent example of the Talmudic method of discovering what the law means by bringing in other statements, similar cases or actual events. All are regularly used by the Rabbis in trying to make clear just what a given law does or does not cover.

CHAPTER 13

Life for life

The acute moral problem of whose life comes first when only one can be saved.

This subject is treated in a number of Talmudic and Midrashic passages. The following examples are not recorded together in one place but all deal with one or another aspect of the question.

A. BABYLONIAN TALMUD, TRACTATE PESAHIM, PAGE 25b

A certain man came to Rava and said to him: "The governor of my town has ordered me to kill someone and has warned me that if I do not do so he will have me killed (what am I to do?)." Rava replied: "Let yourself be killed but do not kill him. How do you know that your blood is redder? Perhaps the blood of that man is redder."

Rava, one of the most renowned Babylonian teachers, died around the year 350. The passage reflects conditions in those days. The governor referred to seems to have been a petty tyrant with powers of life and death over those under his jurisdiction. For some reason he was unable to kill the man who had displeased him so he ordered a Jew to do the foul deed for him (or perhaps he wished to involve the Jew in the deed even though he could have had it carried out by his own men). This Jew wished to know what Jewish law would have him do. Now Jewish law does permit a man to do many things that are otherwise wrong if it is necessary to do so to save his life but, says Rava, it draws the line at murder.

As the great commentator, Rashi, explains, it cannot be right to do this wrong in order to save a life, since in this case a life is lost in any event, namely the life of the victim. The only possible justification for a man killing another in order to save his life would be because his own life is more valuable. But no human being can assess the true value of a human life, so Jewish law cannot possibly accept the argument that the murderer's life is more valuable than that of the victim. As Rava puts it: How do you know that your blood is redder? That you are better than he is? Hence the law forbids murder even if the result is that one's life becomes forfeit.

The commentators point out that this rule may not be compromised. It is not only for a case where both men are more or less of equal stature. Even if one is a great scholar or an extremely good man and the other of little account, it is still forbidden for the one to save his own life by killing the other. For all we know to the contrary, in the eyes of God the intended victim's life may be more significant. In fact, the late Rabbi Kook, once Chief Rabbi of Palestine, ruled that even if a whole group of men were ordered to kill one man otherwise they would lose their lives, they must still refrain from murder. It is not given to men to make such terrible decisions on the value of human life. The only thing to be done is for a man to refrain from murder in all circumstances. (See C)

However, this does not mean that a man may not defend himself. In fact, the Rabbis say elsewhere that if it is clear someone wishes to murder you, you should save your life by killing him. The difference is that in that case he has designs on your life whereas in Rava's case the intended victim is innocent of any such designs. But even where someone wants to kill you, you are not allowed to kill the intended murderer if you can save your life in other ways, by maiming him, for example.

B. SIPHRA ON LEVITICUS 25:36

"That thy brother may live with thee" (Leviticus 25:36). The following was expounded by Ben Petura. Two men were traveling through the desert and one of them has a flask of water. If he alone will drink the water he will reach the town but if both of them drink they will both die. Ben Petura expounded the verse "That thy brother may live with thee" to mean that both should drink and die (rather than that one should live while the other dies). But Rabbi Akiva said to him:

"That thy brother may live with thee" means that your life takes precedence over the life of your friend.

The Siphra from which this passage is taken is one of the
Halakhic Midrashim, a commentary on the book of Leviticus. Apart
from the reference to him in this passage Ben Petura is unknown
in Rabbinic literature, but he was evidently a colleague of the
great Rabbi Akiva mentioned here. Rabbi Akiva lived in the second
century. The case they debate appears to have also been debated
by the Roman lawyers. The question is whether it is better for the man
with the water to drink it all himself and so live until he reaches
a town where he will be provided with food and drink or
to share his water with his companion even though this will mean
that both will die.

It should first be noted that this case is quite different from
the one in A. There the only way the man can save his own life
is by committing murder, but here the man with the water commits
no crime by drinking it himself. Of course, in ordinary circumstances
it would be akin to murder if he refused to give the other man
the water that will save his life, albeit for only a short spell, but
here he needs the water to save his own life. Nonetheless, Ben
Petura argues that since Scripture says "thy brother may live with
thee," it is wrong for the man with the water to refuse to share it
with his companion. His present duty, argues Ben Petura, is
to make his brother "live with him" i.e. to make sure that for the
time being they both live. He must not refrain from acting on his
duty out of considerations of what will later happen to him.

Rabbi Akiva cannot agree with Ben Petura. He interprets the
verse to mean "thy brother may live with thee"; that is to say
where you will live you must see to it that your brother, too, is
allowed to live. That does not mean where your brother's life is
gained, for the time being, at the expense of your own. You do not
need to give your life for his. Later Jewish law follows Rabbi
Akiva arguing that it cannot be right for two lives to be lost if one
can be saved.

It should be noted that neither Rabbi Akiva nor Ben Petura
argue that there is an obligation for the man with the water to give
it to his companion leaving none for himself that his companion
might live even though he perish. There cannot be any such
obligation since if there were it would follow that the companion
once he has the water would have the obligation of giving it back

again! But suppose the man with the water decides that the other man's life is of greater value than his own (e.g. the other man has a wife and children and he has neither) what then? It would seem that while there would be no obligation to do this, it would probably be considered by Judaism as a tremendous act of self-sacrifice if you wished to do so.

C.   TOSEPHTA, TERUMOT, CHAPTER 7:23

If heathen said to a company of men: "Give us one of you that we kill him or else we will kill all of you" they should all let themselves be killed rather than deliver a single soul in Israel. But if they specified a certain person, as they specified Sheba son of Bichri (II Samuel 20:1-22), they should not allow themselves to be killed and should hand him over.

The Tosephta, from which this passage is taken, is a kind of addition or supplement to the Mishnah produced toward the end of the second century. The situation described may often have happened in those days. A group of heathen (robbers or bandits or people who wished to kill a Jew for no reason but blood-lust) come across a small company of Jews and they order them to hand over one of their number for the express purpose of having him murdered. Now to hand over a man to those who intend to murder him is almost the same crime as murder itself and consequently it would have to be compared with Rava's case in A, not with Rabbi Akiva's case in B. Consequently, the Tosephta rules that they must all allow themselves to be killed rather than hand him over. (Even though they will all be killed including the one they might have handed over it is still wrong for them to commit what amounts to the crime of murder.) (It is implied that it would be wrong for them to cast lots to decide which of them should be handed over. You may recall the story of Jonah and the storm when the sailors cast lots.)

However, all this, it is said, only applies if the heathen simply stated that they wanted one of them without any particular preference. But supposing the heathen were bent on killing not just anyone but a particular person in the group. In this case he may be handed over since the heathen are determined to kill him and will, indeed, kill him in any event. Since he had been mentioned specifically by them this is quite different from a group choosing one of their number to be killed to save their own skins. It should in all probability be stated that this only applies where the heathen are so superior in numbers and arms that a straight fight is out of the question. But where a fight is possible, and the group of which the demand is made may win, the law would probably be different since here there is only the risk of death for the other members of the group but certain death for the man picked out.

The story of Sheba son of Bichri is told in the second book of Samuel, chapter 20. Sheba was a rebel against King David. Joab, David's captain, besieged the city in which Sheba had taken refuge and he threatened to destroy the city unless the rebel were handed over to be killed. Advised by an old woman the men of the city cut off Sheba's head and threw it to Joab. From this ancient tale the Tosephta concludes that in the case mentioned above, if the heathen specified a certain man, as Sheba was specified by Joab, it is permitted to hand him over.

D. MISHNAH, HORAYOT, CHAPTER 3:7

A man takes precedence over a woman when it comes to saving a life and to restoring something lost. But a woman takes precedence with regard to the provision of clothes and to be redeemed from captivity.

This case is different from all three mentioned previously. This concerns a person who can save the life of one other when two are clamoring for his help. Supposing for example a man sees two people fall into a swiftly flowing river and he knows that he can only save one of them. Which one should he save? Now in the ordinary way he would have to decide this for himself on the basis of such considerations as whose life he thinks more valuable. (Again it must be said that this case is not to be compared with that of A, in which such an assessment must not be made, for there a crime is committed!) But are there any distinctions between types of persons? The Mishnah rules that a man's life in this case takes precedence over a woman's, and he should save the man first even though this may mean that the woman will drown. This is certainly contrary to our ideas today. Women and children first is the general rule when a ship is going down. But the Rabbis believed that since a man has more religious obligations to fulfill than a woman, he should be saved, not out of any intrinsic virtue which

makes him the superior of a woman, but because he can, if
he lives, have greater opportunities to perform good deeds.

Similarly, the Mishnah rules that if, for instance, a man sees
two animals, one belonging to a man and one belonging to a woman,
both straying far from home and he is only able to catch one
of them, he should give precedence to that of the man. The man
generally in those days was the breadwinner of the family and
his economic soundness was generally held to be more important
for society than that of the woman. If, however, the Mishnah
goes on to say, two poor people, one a man the other a woman,
apply to the charity overseers to be provided with clothes to wear,
the woman comes first, because a woman is far more embarrassed
than a man when she has no suitable clothes to wear. No one
likes to see himself in rags but a man can bear it far more than a
woman can be expected to do. Similarly, the Mishnah rules that
if a man and a woman were held for ransom by bandits and
the community only has enough money to ransom one of them,
they should ransom the woman for the sufferings of a woman in
captivity are far more severe than those of a man.

Sincerity and insincerity in praise

*The laws of telling the truth when one
does not want to hurt people.*

**Our Rabbis taught: How does one sing praises in front of the bride?
The School of Shammai says: A bride as she is. But the School of
Hillel says: A beautiful and graceful bride. Said the School of
Shammai to the School of Hillel: Supposing she was lame or blind
is it right to say of her that she is beautiful and graceful since the
Torah says: "Keep far from falsehood" (Exodus 23:7)? Said the
School of Hillel to the School of Shammai: Consider your own words.
If a man buys something inferior in the market place should people
praise it or disparage it? Surely they should praise it. From this the
Sages derived the rule that a man should always conduct himself
toward others in a pleasant manner.**

*The School (literally the "House") of Shammai and the School
of Hillel flourished almost two thousand years ago in Palestine.
We are told that they debated hundreds of legal matters covering
the whole range of Jewish life. With just a few exceptions later
Jewish law always follows the opinions of the School of Hillel.
Again with just a few exceptions the School of Shammai takes the
stricter view while the School of Hillel is more lenient.*

*This particular debate concerns the question of tact versus truth.
On the one hand Judaism urges us to be truthful and not to tell
lies but sometimes the naked truth can hurt people and Judaism*

also wishes us to avoid, so far as we can, causing hurt to others. It was the custom in those days to sing in front of a bride. A marriage was a great occasion and it was the duty of those present to sing the praises of (literally, dance before) the bride. A usual form of this praise was to declare that the bride is beautiful and graceful. (The word we have translated as "graceful" also suggests "kindliness." The meaning appears to be that the bride is not a haughty beauty but a sweet person.) Now the School of Shammai argues that it is not permitted to say this if it is obviously not true. Supposing the bride is ugly or has a physical defect it is, they argue, not permitted to tell an untruth even out of the best motives. In this case one should be less fulsome in praise of the bride, saying only that which is true. But the School of Hillel argues that it is cruel to suggest to a man, even when he buys something (to say nothing of such an important matter as choosing a wife), that he has made a bad bargain. Why upset him unnecessarily when he can no longer do anything about it? Consequently, it is permitted, and, indeed, necessary, to say that the bride is beautiful and graceful even if she is nothing of the kind. There is the further point that in her husband's eyes she must be beautiful since he has married her. Beauty is a relative term. It is not unknown for people in love to think that their beloved is wonderful in every possible way even though he or she may seem to others to be quite an ordinary person.

When Rav Dimi came (from Palestine to Babylon) he said: This is how they sing in front of the bride in the West (Palestine, which is to the West of Babylon): No eye shadow, no rouge and no lipstick and yet a graceful gazelle.

When the Rabbis ordained Rabbi Zéra they sang for him: No eye shadow, no rouge and no lipstick and yet a graceful gazelle.

Rav Dimi left Palestine to settle in Babylon. He lived in the fourth century and is often reported, as he is here, as conveying Palestinian practices to the Babylonians. The words translated as "No eye shadow" etc. do not mean quite this literally but they all refer to some kind of painting and adornment of a woman and it seemed right to translate it in this way as reflecting conditions as they are today. The Palestinian praise of the bride was that she always looked beautiful even without the benefit of make-up. The Biblical comparison of a beautiful girl to a "gazelle" is made in the Song of Songs.

Rabbi Zéra lived at the end of the third century, first in Babylon, later in Palestine. Ordination was the authority given to a Rabbi to act as such i.e. to give rulings in matters of Jewish law. It may seem odd that the Rabbis sang before Rabbi Zéra at his ordination the song generally reserved for a bride. The meaning would seem to to be that just as a beautiful bride needs no artificial aids to beauty a true scholar like Rabbi Zéra does not need artificial means to impress others. His scholarship is sufficiently impressive in itself. In other passages in the Talmud it is stated that, for example, scholars would sometimes dress up in flowing, splendid robes to show how important they were. Men like Rabbi Zéra, it is implied, do not need to do this. Their learning speaks for them. We can imagine a college President today conferring a high degree on a retiring, perhaps shabbily dressed scholar, remarking that a beautiful bride needs no artificial aids to beauty. There is the further point that frequently in Rabbinic literature the Torah is spoken of as Israel's bride so that by an association of ideas it would be natural to slip into this kind of metaphor when speaking of a man learned in the Torah.

When the Rabbis ordained Rabbi Ammi and Rabbi Assi they sang for them: Like these, only like these, ordain for us. Do not ordain for us the confused thinkers or the ragged thinkers. Others say (that the Rabbis said): No second-rate scholars and no third-rate scholars.

Rabbi Ammi and Rabbi Assi both lived in the third century in Palestine and are generally mentioned together as close friends and, it seems, they were also near relatives. Some think that, in fact, they were brothers. They were ordained together. The terms used in the song sung for them are very unusual terms and the commentators are not too sure what they mean but it is hoped that the translation given of the text conveys approximately the meaning of these terms. It is clear from this and from other Talmudic passages that it sometimes happened that people who were really unworthy fooled the examiners and managed to get themselves ordained. The Rabbis who ordained Rabbi Ammi and Rabbi Assi saw fit, while singing their praises, to protest against unworthy ordinations.

When Rabbi Abbahu came from the college to Caesar's house the maidservants of Caesar's house came out to meet him and sang to him: Head of his people and leader of his nation, candelabra of light, let thy coming be in peace.

Rabbi Abbahu was a Palestinian scholar of the late third and the fourth century. He eventually became the head of the college at Caesarea. The reference to Caesar's house here is not, of course, to the Imperial palace in Rome but probably to the house of the Roman pro-consul at Caesarea. It might be mentioned that in the Rabbinic tradition Rabbi Abbahu was one of the most handsome men who ever lived, which would explain the extravagant praise of him by the maids of the house.

They said regarding Rabbi Judah son of Ilai that he used to take a twig of myrtle and dance in front of the bride saying: A beautiful and graceful bride. Rav Samuel son of Rav Isaac used to dance (in front of the bride) juggling with three twigs. Rabbi Zéra said: The old man is causing us embarrassment. When he died a pillar of fire came down to act as a barrier between him and the people and we have a tradition that this only happens to one in a generation or to two in a generation. Rabbi Zéra said: His twig helped the old man. Others say (that Rabbi Zéra said): His attitude helped the old man. Others say (Rabbi Zéra said): His folly helped the old man.

Rabbi Judah son of Ilai was one of the most famous Palestinian scholars of the second century, a pupil of the great Rabbi Akiva and renowned for his piety. Myrtle twigs were widely used in those days for their fragrance and for adorning homes. Rav Samuel son of Rav Isaac lived at the end of the third century in both Palestine and Babylon. The actual text says that "he danced with three" which the commentators take to mean that in dancing in front of the bride he juggled with three myrtle leaves in order to delight the bride and her company. Rabbi Zéra did not approve of this levity, feeling it to be undignified for a scholar. The legend of a pillar of fire coming down at the funeral of a great man to act as a barrier is very old. It was said that this happened only for the most outstanding men of their generation, for one or at the most two in each generation. Since this is said to have happened at Rabbi Samuel's funeral Rabbi Zéra saw it as a sign of divine approval of Rabbi Samuel's conduct.

There are three versions of what Rabbi Zéra actually said. The point here is that there are three words with very similar sounds. These are: shot, "a twig"; shitah, "an attitude"; and shoteh, "a fool." Hence there are three versions: either "his twig" or "his attitude" or "his folly," the latter meaning being that even though what he did appeared to be an act of folly it was accepted as being in a good cause.

CHAPTER 15

BABYLONIAN TALMUD, TRACTATE BAVA BATRA, PAGES 6b–7a

A man's property and his inconvenience

The laws of property rights which conflict
with the desires of others.

The Rabbis appearing in this discussion are: Rav Ḥama (fourth century); Rabbah (third and early fourth centuries); Rav Naḥman (third and early fourth centuries); Mar Zutra his son; and Rav Huna son of Rav Joshua (fourth century); all of them Babylonian teachers. Rav Naḥman was renowned as a famous judge in whose name various decisions were repeated. But these were sometimes stated wrongly hence Rabbah here corrects what he considers to be an incorrect report of what Rav Naḥman said.

The basic question discussed here is how far can a man reasonably exercise his rights to his property even when these interfere with his neighbor's comfort and even when the neighbor offers adequate compensation.

Two men were living in a house, one on the upper floor, one on the ground floor. The ground floor began to sink into the earth whereupon the owner of the ground floor said to the owner of the upper floor: Let us rebuild the house. He replied: I can live quite well where I am. He then said to him: Very well I shall pay for the demolition of the house and for its rebuilding. He said: But I have nowhere to live in the meantime. He replied: I shall rent a house for you. He

replied: I do not want to bother. He said: But I cannot live like this. He said: Crawl in on your stomach and crawl out on your stomach. Rav Ḥama said: He has every right in law to prevent the demolition of the house.

Here we have a case of two men, one owning the ground floor of a house, one the top floor. In those days most houses consisted of two large rooms (subdivided into smaller compartments) one on ground level, the other above it. It was, incidentally, very unusual to have an indoor staircase. The top floor was generally reached either by a ladder or by an outside staircase. It was usual, and there are many references to this in the Talmud, for one man to own and live in the large room on the ground floor and another to own and live in the large room on the top floor.

The soil in Babylon was fairly soft and house-building being what it was in those days it was not infrequent for the walls to begin to sink into the ground after a time. This happened in our case with the result that the owner of the ground floor found that his living space was being reduced until he felt moved to do something about it. The only thing possible was to demolish the whole building and rebuild it, and for this permission had naturally to be obtained from the owner of the top floor. In all probability we have here the actual arguments these two men presented when the case came before the courts.

The owner of the top floor argues that he has no need to rebuild because his roominess is not affected and he can live quite comfortably where he is. The ground floor owner acknowledged that it would be unreasonable for him to expect the other man to share the expenses, and offers to foot the whole bill himself. But, the other man goes on to argue, where will I live while the old house is being demolished and the new one built? I will pay for the rent of the apartment in which you will stay, replies the ground floor man. To which the top floor man replies that he does not want to be bothered to move. But, argues the ground floor man, how can I live in such a restricted space. That is your worry, says the top floor man in so many words; you must crawl in and crawl out as best you can. Is it right that the top floor man should obstruct the wishes of the ground floor man in this way? Rav Hama rules that he has every right to refuse to be cooperative. Of course, it would be pleasant if he decided to help his neighbor and cooperate, but the law cannot interfere to compel him to do so since he is doing no *wrong. This does not mean that a man can exercise his rights to be a public nuisance. If, for instance, he had a smoking chimney the law could compel him to have it attended to, but in our case his property causes no nuisance in itself and the law cannot touch him.*

But this only applies where the walls of the ground floor do not sink lower than ten handbreadths from the earth, but if they sink as low as this the owner of the ground floor can say: Lower than ten hand-breadths from the earth is my domain and you have no right to be there.

However, it is stated, this only applied if the beams of the ceiling do not come down so low as ten handbreadths from the floor, but if they do come down as low as this the top floor man is, in fact, invading the domain of the ground floor man and this he has no right to do. The point here is that the ownership of the ground floor is determined by law as consisting of not alone the actual space from floor to ceiling but the space of ten handbreadths from the ground.

And furthermore the right of the owner of the top floor to object only applies if they had made no conditions at the beginning, but if they had made conditions at the beginning (that if the house begins to sink they would both rebuild it) they must both be prepared to rebuild it.

It is further stated that all this only applies where the two bought their respective dwellings unconditionally. But, of course, it is open to them at the beginning to divide up the dwelling space conditionally. And if a condition were made right at the beginning that in the event of the walls sinking they will both be responsible, then it is obvious that the owner of the top floor must contribute toward the cost of the new dwelling.

If they did make conditions, how deep has the ground floor to sink before the owner can demand that the house be rebuilt? The Rabbis said to Rabbah in the name of Mar Zutra son of Rav Naḥman who said it in the name of Rav Naḥman: It should follow the rule we have learned: "Its height should be equal to half its length and half its breadth together." Rabbah said to them: Have I not told you that

you must not hang empty bottles on Rav Naḥman? This is, in fact, what Rav Naḥman said: It must be big enough for him to live in it in the way in which people generally live in houses. And how much is that? Rav Huna son of Rav Joshua said: It must be big enough for some reeds of Maḥoza to be brought into it and turned around in it.

But this requires some further elaboration. For surely it would be unreasonable for the law to compel the top floor man to contribute if the ground floor walls only sank a little. How much, then, have they to sink for the demand to rebuild to be legal?

The Rabbis reported to Rabbah in the name of Mar Zutra the son of Rav Naḥman that the famous judge Rav Naḥman had ruled in such cases that the demand can be legally made if the ceiling has sunk so low that the height of the ground floor dwelling is less than the sum total of half its length and half its breadth. This is based on a ruling found later in this Tractate. Here it is stated that if a builder undertakes to build someone a house (i.e. of one floor only), and there have been no specifications as to height, the purchaser has a case in law if the builder made the height less than the sum total of half the length and half the breadth. From which it appears that a normal house or room is expected to be at least of these dimensions.

Rabbah, however, objects that Rav Naḥman has been inaccurately reported. In the idiom of the day, "empty bottles" had been hung on him i.e. unsound opinions had been attributed to him. The true size for the demand to be legally made is when the house or room becomes so low that there is no room to swing around in it the long reeds which grew near the town of Maḥoza on the river Tigris. It seems that in those days the expression for a small room was a place in which there was no room to swing around the reeds of Maḥoza (compare our idiom: no room to swing a cat). Since people do not normally dwell in a room lower than this, the ground floor man can invoke the condition made at the beginning if the walls of his floor sink to this extent.

A man once began to build a wall facing his neighbor's windows. He said to him: You will make it dark for me. He replied: Very well, I shall close these windows up for you and make new windows for you higher than my wall. He replied: No, this will spoil my wall. He said: Very well, I shall demolish the wall in your house as far as the windows go and then I shall build you a new wall and make windows in it higher than my wall. He said: A wall that is new on top and old at the bottom will not stand firmly. He replied: Very well I shall demolish the whole wall and rebuild it with windows. He said: No, one new wall in an old house will not stand firmly. He replied: Very well, I shall demolish the whole house and build you a new one with windows in it. He replied: I have nowhere to live in the meantime. He replied: I shall hire a house for you. He said: I do not want the bother. Rav Hama said: He has every right in law to prevent it.

Another similar case is now reported. The law is clear that a man can legally prevent another from building a wall which will obstruct his light by blocking the light from entering his windows. (This is the law of "ancient lights" in many countries.) But when this legal right was claimed by the man with the windows the man intending to build the obstructing wall offered to make himself responsible for rebuilding the wall in which the windows were built and to rebuild it with the windows higher than the obstruction. To this the window man objects that the reconstruction will spoil his walls because the new windows will have to be knocked out of the wall. Very well then, replies the wall man, I will build a new wall on that part. No, replies the window man, because this will be a new wall on top of the old part and this will not last very long. Very well, then, I will build you a completely new wall. No, because then there will be one new wall in an old house and the whole structure will be in danger. Very well, then, I will build you a new house. No, because I have nowhere to live for the time being. I will obtain a house for you for the time being. I do not want to be bothered. Rav Hama again rules that this is a legitimate reply and the window man can legally prevent the wall man from proceeding with his building project.

But are not these two cases exactly the same and why is it necessary to repeat it? It is necessary for us to know that even if the house is only used as a store for straw and wood he can still prevent its demolition.

The final question is raised as to why it is necessary for the Talmud to record the two rulings of Rav Hama (the one about the two floors and the one about the wall and the windows). Since the same principle is involved in both cases would we not be able to deduce the second case from the ruling in the first? To this the answer is given that if the second case were deduced from the first we would think that the law only applies where the window man lives himself in the house (as in the two floors case). But where he only uses the house for storage we might have argued that it cannot be too inconvenient to store his wood and straw elsewhere for the time being. Hence the second case is quoted to demonstrate that he has a right to object even if he only uses the house for storage purposes.

CHAPTER 16

BABYLONIAN TALMUD, TRACTATE PESAḤIM, PAGES 8a–b

Doing good deeds despite danger

The laws for doing good deeds where there is danger
and the motive for doing good deeds.

It was taught: "He is not obliged to put his hand into holes and cracks in a wall searching for leaven because of the danger." What danger? If the danger is from snakes how could he have used the wall for the purpose in the first place? The wall fell in after he had used it. But if the wall fell in why search for leaven there, have we not been taught: "If a wall falls upon leaven the leaven is treated as if it had been destroyed"? That refers to when the leaven is so deeply buried that a dog cannot dig it out whereas here we deal with leaven that a dog can dig out. But did not Rabbi Eleazar say that people engaged in the performance of a good deed will come to no harm? Rav Ashi said: He might lose a needle and look for it at the same time. Does this mean that in that case it would not be a good deed? Have we not been taught: If a man says: "This *sela* for charity on condition that my son lives or that I am a son of the world to come" he is altogether righteous? He might look for the needle after he has searched for the leaven.

The Mishnah teaches that on the night before Passover it is necessary to search for leaven in one's house. Any leaven must be destroyed before Passover because no leaven must be in the house during the festival. However, the Mishnah rules, this only applies to places in which leaven is brought during the rest of the year. No search is required in a place into which leaven is not normally brought.

In those days it was usual for people to leave bread and other food in cracks or holes in the walls of the house. Consequently, it might have been thought necessary to search in these cracks for leaven. But the Baraita (a source from the period of the Mishnah) rules that this should not be done because there is danger in so doing. The Talmud then asks: What is the nature of this danger, what can there be so dangerous in putting one's hand into a crack in a wall? The answer is that the danger is from snakes in the wall who may bite the searcher. But, the Talmud objects, if it is a wall where there is danger from snakes how could he have used it for leaven in the first place? If he did not, then in any event he would not have to search for leaven there. To this the reply is given that he used the wall while it was still standing and then there was no danger from snakes who could not get into the wall. But now the wall has fallen in and there is that danger. But, objects the Talmud further, if the wall has fallen in he is not obliged to search for leaven there. That is because the Mishnah rules that if a wall falls on top of leaven the leaven is treated as if it were already destroyed since no one can normally get at it. The answer is given that the rule regarding leaven under a fallen wall only applies to a wall so thick that, after it has fallen, a dog cannot dig up the leaven. We are dealing with a wall not so thick and here it would have been necessary to search for the leaven were it not for the danger from snakes.

It follows from what has been said that although there is a duty to search for leaven this duty should not be carried out in circumstances which are dangerous. But the Talmud now objects that Rabbi Eleazar (third century, Palestine) said that anyone engaged in carrying out a good deed need not be afraid that he will come to harm then because God will protect him. In that case let him search for the leaven and as for the danger from snakes, God will protect him. Rav Ashi (fifth century, Babylon) replies to this that the guarantee only applies while he is performing the good deed from the right motive. But in our case since he is looking for the leaven he might think to himself that at the same time he might as well look for something else he might have lost during the year, a needle for example. In that case his motive is not pure. His search is not for the sake of doing the good deed alone, and therefore the protection afforded to one who does a good deed is not provided here. But the Talmud objects that it is wrong to argue that a selfish motive is sufficient to cancel out the good deed. A good deed is still a good deed even if the motive for which it is done is not exactly right. Hence even if at the same time he looks for a needle and so forth, he is still doing a good deed and is afforded protection. In support of this a Baraita is quoted. Here it is stated that if a man gives a sela (the name of a coin—worth four zuz) to charity but says at the time of giving that he wants God to bless his son or to give him a share in Paradise in return for his charity, he is still a good man even though his motive is selfish. So the man should be allowed to search for lost objects like a needle while he is searching for the leaven. The Talmud answers that this would be all right. But if he were allowed to do them simultaneously he might go on to look for the needle after he has done the good deed of searching for leaven. In that case he would be placing himself in danger without performing a good deed and there would be no protection. Consequently, he is freed altogether from the obligation of searching because he may be led into danger.

Rav Naḥman son of Isaac said: The danger is that of gentiles and this follows the opinion of Pelimo. For we have been taught: "If there is a hole in a wall between a Jew and a gentile he should search for leaven as far into the hole as his hand reaches and should nullify the rest in his heart. Pelimo said: He does not have to search for it at all in this case because of the danger." What danger? If you will argue that the danger is of suspicions of magic, in that case how did he use the hole in the wall in the first instance? When he used it in the first instance it was daytime and there would be no reason for suspecting him of magic, but now it is night time and he is using a candle and there would be reason to suspect him of magic. But did not Rabbi Eleazar say that people engaged in the performance of good deeds will come to no harm? Yes, but the situation is different in cases where the harm is likely to occur, for it is said: "And Samuel said: How can I go? If Saul will hear it, he will kill me. And the Lord said: Take a heifer with thee." (I Samuel 16:2)

The Talmud now gives a new version of the whole argument. Up to now we have been assuming that the danger is from snakes. Rav Naḥman son of Isaac (third century, Babylon) states that the danger is from his gentile neighbor, and in support the opinion of Pelimo is quoted. (Pelimo was a second century teacher in Palestine.) The first opinion in the Baraita quoted is that in the case of a hole between a Jewish and gentile house the Jew should search as far as he can and then nullify the rest in his heart i.e. he should give up his ownership of any leaven which may be left in the hole. Once a man has given up his ownership of any leaven it is no longer his and may be kept in the house. But Pelimo argues that since there is danger to the Jew he should not search at all in this case. The danger, says the Talmud, is that the gentile will think that the Jew is casting a magic spell on him and he may retaliate. (It should not be forgotten that in those days there was a good deal of superstition about the people were genuinely afraid of spells and the like.) But the Talmud objects that in that case how did he use the hole in the first place without arousing suspicion of doing magic. The obvious answer is given that there is all the difference in the world between using the hole openly by day and looking into it, seemingly stealthily, by night with a candle (required for searching for the leaven). Here again the objection is put forward that Rabbi Eleazar said that the good deed is a protection against harm. This time the answer is given that Rabbi Eleazar only states that protection is afforded where the danger is remote. But where the danger is likely to happen it may happen even while a good deed is being carried out. (If this were not so it would mean that God would be obliged to perform a miracle in protecting the man and miracles are not so easily performed.) As proof of this the case of the prophet Samuel is quoted. Even though God had told Samuel to go to David, Samuel was afraid that David would kill him. Samuel evidently did not rely on the protection afforded by the good deed (of obeying God's command) because there was a near danger, not a remote one.

They asked Rav: What of the scholars who live out in the country? May they come in the early morning or late at night to the college? He replied: Let them come and on me and my neck be it. What of them returning? He said: This I do not know. It has been said: Rabbi Eleazar said: People engaged in the performance of good deeds will come to harm neither in going nor in returning. With whom does this agree? With the following teacher, for we have been taught: Isi son of Judah said: Since the Torah says "No man shall desire thy land" (Exodus 34:24), it means that your cow will graze in the meadow and no beast will harm it; your fowl will scratch in the dungheap and no weasel will harm it. Now it is an argument from the lesser to the greater. If these which naturally come to harm are not harmed then human beings who are not naturally harmed how much more so! I know only that there will be no harm in going. How do I know that the same applies to returning? Because Scripture says: "And thou shalt turn in the morning, and go unto thy tents" (Deuteronomy 16:7). This means that you will go and find your tent in peace. But if no harm will come to him even in returning surely it follows that no harm will come in going and why should a verse be required for this? The verse is required to teach Rabbi Ammi's teaching, for Rabbi Ammi said: A man who has land is obliged to go up on pilgrimage but a man who has no land is not obliged to go up on pilgrimage.

Rav was the famous third century teacher in Babylon. He was asked whether the students at the college may come to their lessons during the night or early morning. In those days of robbers and wild beasts it was a little hazardous to journey by night. Rav replies that he was prepared to take full responsibility. He evidently agreed with his contemporary Rabbi Eleazar that good deeds are a safeguard. They then asked Rav if he was equally confident that they would not come to harm while returning at night or in the early morning. Rav replied that of this he was not so sure because here it might be argued that once they had carried out the good deed (of studying) the protection of the good deed no longer applied. However, the complete saying of Rabbi Eleazar is now quoted and in this he stated clearly that even on their return from doing the good deed they will not come to harm. The reasoning here appears to be that if they would be afraid of coming to harm on their return they would not go in the first place so that the return, too, is part of the good deed.

In support of Rabbi Eleazar the teaching of Isi (second century, Palestine) is quoted. Isi is commenting on the verse which states that when people go up to Jerusalem on pilgrimage three times a year they need not be afraid of anything happening to their land. This is taken to mean that they are promised that none of their animals will be harmed. Now animals are easily harmed and yet the promise is made so that it can be argued (from the lesser to the greater) that they themselves will not come to harm while going on pilgrimage. And as for their returning, another verse is quoted which teaches that they will come home in peace.

We now have two verses. The first promises that no harm will come to them when they set out, the second that no harm will come to them on their return. But if they are promised that no harm will come to them until their return, is it not obvious that no harm will come to them when they go? The answer is given that really no verse is required and the real purpose of the first verse (which speaks of "land") is quite the other. It is to teach that only a person with land of his own is obliged to go on the pilgrimage. Rabbi Ammi, in fact, said just this.

Rabbi Avin son of Rabbi Adda said in the name of Rabbi Isaac: Why are there no fruits of *Gennesaret* in Jerusalem? So that the pilgrims should not say: "Had we merely gone up for no other purpose than to enjoy the fruits of *Gennesaret* in Jerusalem it would have been enough" and their pilgrimage would not then have been for its own sake. Similarly, Rabbi Dosetai son of Rabbi Jannai said: Why are the hot springs of Tiberias not found in Jerusalem? So that the pilgrims should not say: "Had we merely gone up for no other purpose than to enjoy the hot springs of Tiberias it would have been enough" and their pilgrimage would not then have been for its own sake.

The passage concludes with some further observations by third and second century teachers. Since the previous discussion refers to a good deed carried out with selfish motives the relevance of this passage can be seen. The fruits of Gennesaret (Kinneret) are the fruits grown near the shores of Lake Tiberias and at Tiberias, too, were the famous hot springs. The question is raised why did God not make Jerusalem to have these luxuries and benefits. The answer is given that if there were too many comforts in Jerusalem people may not go there simply to carry out the obligation of going on pilgrimage but might go there for the sake of the physical benefits.

When there is doubt about an estate

The laws of an estate of doubtful ownership.

A certain person deposited seven pearls wrapped in a cloth with Rabbi Me'asha the grandson of Rabbi Joshua son of Levi. Rabbi Me'asha died without leaving a will. The case came before Rabbi Ammi. Rabbi Ammi said: For one thing we know that Rabbi Me'asha, the grandson of Rabbi Joshua son of Levi, was not a rich man. Furthermore he has given clear indications that the property belongs to him. This only applies to a case where he did not go regularly into his house. But where he went regularly into his house it is possible that someone else had deposited the property there and he simply saw it.

A certain person deposited a silver cup with Hasa. Hasa died without leaving a will. The case came before Rav Nahman. Rav Nahman said: We know that Hasa was not a rich man. Furthermore he has given clear indications that the property belongs to him. This only applies to a case where he did not go regularly into his house. But where he went regularly into his house it is possible that someone else had deposited the property there and he simply saw it.

A certain person deposited a silken cloak with Rav Dimi brother of Rav Saphra. Rav Dimi died without leaving a will. The case came before Rabbi Abba. He said: For one thing we know that Rav Dimi was not a rich man. Furthermore he has given clear indications that the property belongs to him. This only applies where he did not go regularly into his house. But where he went regularly into his house

**it is possible that someone else had deposited the property there
and he simply saw it.**

This passage first gives an account of three cases all with the same
principles involved, which actually happened. The judges were:
Rabbi Ammi (third century, Palestine) in the first case, Rav Naḥman
(third century, Babylon) in the second, and Rabbi Abba (fourth
century, Palestine) in the third. It is possible that the decision was
well known in the various courts and is not the original decision of
the three judges. This would account for the almost identical
wording in all three cases. Note the names Rabbi Me'asha grandson
of Rabbi Joshua son of Levi and Rav Dimi brother of Rav Saphra.
Normally names follow the father but here Rabbi Joshua and Rav
Saphra were particularly famous so that the grandson in the one case,
the brother in the other, were called after these famous men.

 All three cases concern a man who died without leaving a will
and without sorting out his property before he died. He had no
chance of telling his heirs if he had in his possession property
belonging to another. Now in any ordinary case a person who claimed
to have some property in the possession of another would be
obliged to prove his case with conclusive evidence. Here the heirs
themselves cannot state with confidence that the man who comes and
asks has no claim. Moreover, he does know enough about the
objects supposedly deposited to be able to describe them.
Therefore, the three judges all rule that the claim is legitimate for
two reasons. First the dead man in question was too poor to own the
costly object claimed. Hence it is extremely likely that it was not, in
fact, his own but deposited with him because he was considered
a trustworthy person. Secondly, there is some evidence that the man
making the claim is telling the truth, otherwise how would he know
the details of the object deposited i.e. in the first case, that there
were seven pearls wrapped in a cloth? It follows that if only one of
these reasons were present the object would not be handed over.
If, for example, the heirs were those of a rich man, it could be
argued that without more definite proof they are entitled to conclude
that the object belonged to him. Or if the man making the claim
were able to discover the details of the object deposited this would
obviously afford no proof. Thus, the account concludes in each case
that if the man making the claim used to visit regularly the house
of the dead man there is no indication of ownership because he
might have seen the object there on his frequent visits.

A certain person said on his deathbed: My property should be given to Tobiah, and then he died. Tobiah came to claim the property. Rabbi Joḥanan said: Behold Tobiah has come.

The next case discussed is similarly one in which there is doubt concerning property because a man has died without clarifying the matter. It appears that this was an actual case which came before the third century teacher in Palestine, Rabbi Joḥanan. The case was one in which a man on his deathbed said to witnesses: I wish to give my property to Tobiah. They testified in the court that he had said this and all that remained was to identify Tobiah. Eventually a man called Tobiah actually appeared and when he heard of the last request of the man who had departed claimed that it was he who was meant. Rabbi Joḥanan ruled that he had a right to the property. "Behold Tobiah has come," said Rabbi Joḥanan, as if to say, what more evidence can be required? The dead man did mention the name of Tobiah, a man called Tobiah has come to make the claim.

If he said "Tobiah" and Rabbi Tobiah came, then he said: "Tobiah" not "to *Rabbi* Tobiah." But if he was very familiar with him then out of familiarity he called him "Tobiah."

If two men came, both called "Tobiah," then if one was a neighbor and the other a scholar, the scholar comes first. If one was a relative and the other a scholar, the scholar comes first. They asked: What is the law if one was a relative and the other a neighbor? Come and hear: "Better is a neighbor that is near than a brother far off" (Proverbs 27:10).

If both were relatives or both neighbors or both scholars it is left to the court to decide to whom the property should be given.

There now follows some purely theoretical cases based on the original actual case of Tobiah and Rabbi Joḥanan. Supposing the man who came was not called simply Tobiah but Rabbi Tobiah i.e. he was a scholar and everyone added the title when speaking of him. Then in that case it can be assumed that if the dead man had meant him he would have used the title. However, if he was a great friend of the scholar it can be assumed that it was the scholar that he meant and the reason he used the name on its own was because he was so close to his friend as to make it absurd to use the title.

Supposing two men came, both called Tobiah? Then the ruling is that if one of them is a scholar it can be assumed that he was intended since it was considered to be a religious duty to help scholars financially in order that they might have time to study the Torah.

They (that is, the scholars in the college) asked this question: If there were two men both called Tobiah but one was a relative and one a neighbor, which of them did he have in mind? A verse from the book of Proverbs is quoted according to which a good neighbor is better than a brother who is distant; consequently it can be assumed that since he did not specify which Tobiah he meant it can be assumed that he meant the neighbor, not the relative.

Finally, the question is raised: What if there is no way of deciding which of the two men is meant; if, for example, they were both scholars or both neighbors or both relatives? In that case since there is no hard and fast rule for determining which of the two has the true claim, it is left to the court to decide. Some of the medieval commentators argue that in such a case the court can decide to give the property to the one it favors without having any reason for favoring this one rather than that. But the famous French commentator Rashi and also Maimonides hold that this cannot be law. It is impossible that the court should be empowered to act in an arbitrary way and give away someone's property to a man the court favors without adequate reason. Therefore Rashi and Maimonides understand the ruling here to mean that it is left to the court to go into the case as carefully as it can by such means as interviewing people who knew the dead man well in order to discover which of the two men he is likely to have meant.

CHAPTER 18

First option in the sale of real estate

The special rights of a neighbor when real estate is up for sale.

This lengthy passage concerns the law of bar metzra, "the son of the boundary" (this is the literal translation) which we have translated as "the law of first option." The principle is that although a man can, legally speaking, do as he pleases with his own land the Rabbis considered it unreasonable for a man to deprive the owner of a neighboring field of the possibility of owning two adjacent fields. Obviously it is more convenient to have two fields adjoining one another. They are easier to work and many expenses are saved. Consequently, the first option on the sale is given to the owner of the neighboring field. That is to say if A is about to sell a field and B, who has a field next to the one to be sold, is prepared to offer him the price he is asking, he must sell it to B rather than anyone else. According to many authorities the same law would apply to two adjoining houses, which can be made into one large house.

Rav Judah said in the name of Rav: If someone takes possession of some land lying among fields which belong to brothers or partners it is impudent but he cannot be removed from there. But Rav Naḥman said: He can be removed from there. If, however, the surrounding fields did not belong to brothers or partners but an attempt is made to remove him on the grounds of the law of first option he cannot

be removed. But the scholars of Nehardea say that even on these grounds he can be removed because Scripture says: "And thou shalt do that which is right and good in the sight of the Lord" (Deuteronomy 6:18).

The whole discussion is introduced with a ruling by Rav Judah in the name of his teacher Rav, both of whom lived in Babylon in the third century, as did Rav Naḥman and the scholars of Nehardea mentioned in this section. Nehardea was a town in Babylon situated on the river Euphrates. There was a good deal of scholarly activity there. The "scholars of Nehardea" mentioned later in the passage belonged to a later generation. Rav's ruling was as follows. If a man bought a field surrounded by land belonging to brothers who had inherited the whole surrounding area, or to partners who owned jointly the surrounding area, it is an impudent thing that he has done. The Rabbis frown on such a deal because the option should be given to the brothers or partners to buy the field in the middle and so add it to their joint ownership. However, said Rav, if he did buy the field he cannot be evicted by law. Rav Naḥman disagrees and argues that he can be evicted by law. But Rav Naḥman goes on to say that the law of first option does not apply, that is if the surrounding fields are owned by people other than brothers or partners; or, in any event, not to the extent of having the buyer evicted and the sale rendered invalid. The scholars of Nehardea, and they are followed, rule, however, that he can be evicted because of the law of first option. They quote the verse about doing that which is right and good. They take this to mean that even if there is no actual law on the books against unfair dealing of this sort such a law must be introduced. It is only right and fair that the owner of the neighboring field should have the first option and this means that even after the field has been sold he has the right to pay to the buyer of the field the amount the said buyer paid for it, thus acquiring it for himself.

Supposing the man desiring to buy the field first consulted the owner of the neighboring field who told him to go ahead and buy, is it necessary for the prospective buyer to acquire that right formally or not? Rabina said: No formal act is necessary but the scholars of Nehardea say that a formal act is necessary. The law is that a formal act is necessary.

Even though it has been established that the owner of the neighboring field has first option he can, of course, refuse to avail himself of it. A man, wishing to make sure that the sale will be valid, consults, therefore, the owner of the neighboring field and obtains permission to buy the land up for sale. The question is whether the owner of the neighboring field can go back on the permission he has given and later claim his first option. Now, in normal cases, a mere verbal understanding is not valid in law and it is necessary to perform a formal act to establish any right to property. This formal act is known as a kinyan, literally "an acquisition." For example, a man buying something nowadays might signify consent by shaking hands on the deal, and this is the kinyan. Can the owner of the neighboring field go back on his word if he had not made a kinyan? The late fourth century teacher Rabina said that here verbal consent is sufficient, but the scholars of Nehardea disagreed. The Talmud concludes that the law follows the scholars of Nehardea and hence the owner of the neighboring field can go back on his word unless, of course, a kinyan had been made. The commentators explain that the owner of the neighboring field can claim that although he gave permission for the man to buy the field, this was only because he did not wish the seller to know that he was interested because if the seller knew that an owner of a neighboring field wanted it he would push the price up.

Now that the law is that a formal act is necessary then if no such act had taken place any increase or fall in the value of the land is said to take place in the ownership of the neighbor, not the prospective buyer.

Since the owner of the neighboring field has the right to buy it from the buyer as long as there was no formal act giving up this right, then he is considered as the original buyer. Hence if the price went up after the sale to the buyer he need only pay him the amount he paid for it, as if he had bought it in the first instance. Conversely, if the price went down after the original sale he must pay the first buyer the amount he paid for it, not the present price.

Supposing the buyer bought the field for a hundred zuz but it is really worth two hundred: Then we must look into the matter. If the seller would have sold it to anyone at this price of a hundred then the

owner of the neighboring field has to give the buyer one hundred
zuz and he can then take it for himself. But if the buyer only sold it
at the cheap price as a favor to this particular buyer then the owner
of the neighboring field must give the buyer two hundred zuz and he
can then take it for himself.

*This takes up further the case of an original buyer who now has
to resell it to the owner of the neighboring field. Supposing he
obtained the field at less than the market price. Then it
all depends. If the seller simply wishes to ignore the market price
and sell it cheap to anyone who wishes to buy, then the
owner of the neighboring field need only pay the low price the first
buyer paid. But if the seller only accepted a low price as a favor
to the first buyer then the owner of the neighboring field must
pay the first buyer the full market price.*

Supposing the buyer bought the field for two hundred and it is only
worth one hundred, then at first they thought that the owner of the
neighboring field can say: "I sent you for my benefit not to harm
me," but Mar Kashisha son of Rav Ḥisda said to Rav Ashi: The
scholars of Nehardea said in the name of Rav Naḥman: The laws
regarding overcharging do not apply to land.

*If the buyer paid too much for the field, is the owner of the
neighboring field obliged to give him the amount he paid even
though it is far beyond the market price? At first the scholars thought
that the first buyer is to be treated as a kind of agent of the
owner of the neighboring field. Now if A sent B to be his agent to
buy something for him and he paid too much, B would have
to pay the difference. However it was said to the famous late fourth
century teacher Rav Ashi that there had been an earlier rule that
with regard to land one cannot render a sale invalid even if there
is a large overcharge. Hence even though the first buyer paid
far too much for the field it is still considered to be a fair price.
The reason why the rules regarding overcharge do not apply to land
is that the Sages believe land is always worth what is paid for it.*

If a man bought a *geriva* of land in the middle of the land he
intends to buy, then we must look into the matter. If the small
portion of land he bought was of very good quality or very bad the
sale is a valid one, otherwise it is merely a trick.

A geriva *is a very small portion of land. Supposing a man bought a small portion of this size, are we to be afraid that it is only a trick to make him, too, an owner of a neighboring portion of land so that he can later buy a large field to which otherwise he would not be entitled? If it is a trick then the sale is invalid. The test is given that if the small portion is either very good land or very bad (and in this it is different from all surrounding land) then there is nothing unusual in its being sold separately and it is a genuine and hence valid sale. But if not then it is only a trick and the sale is invalid.*

The law of first option does not apply to a gift. Amemar said: If he wrote out a bill granting security to the person to whom the gift was given then the law of first option does apply.

Obviously the law of first option does not apply to a gift. If A wishes to give B a field, C, the owner of a neighboring field, cannot claim the right of first option. This is obvious. A does not wish to sell the field at all but to give it away to B. If, however, he wrote out for the benefit of B a document in which he states that if anyone later took the field from B (e.g. in payment of a debt which A owes) then he, A, will give him another field, we can assume that the gift was not really a gift but a secret sale since no one gives such a bill of security for a field given as a gift.

The law of first option does not apply if a man sold all his property to another.

If a man sold all his property to another and this included a field over which a neighbor would normally have first option, he would not have it here since the seller gains in many ways by a complete sale of all his property. The rule of fairness only applies where there is no financial loss to the seller or first buyer.

The law of first option does not apply if a man sold a field to its previous owner.

The previous owner would like to have his old field back again and to sell it back to him is more an act of fairness than to sell it to the owner of the neighboring field.

The law of first option does not apply if a man bought a field from a heathen or sold a field to a heathen. In the case where he bought it from a heathen the law does not apply because the buyer can say to the owner of the neighboring field: I have chased a lion away from your boundary. In the case where he sold it to a heathen the law does not apply because the command to do that which is right and good cannot be imposed on a heathen. Nevertheless, the seller is placed under a ban until he accepts upon himself full responsibility from any harm that may be caused by the proximity of the heathen.

This paragraph has to be understood against the background of those times when the heathen peoples frequently took advantage of the minority status of the Jews. It was unpleasant and frequently harmful for a Jewish farmer to have a close heathen neighbor. Consequently, a field bought from a heathen is excluded from the law of first option because the buyer can say to the owner of the neighboring field: Far from doing you any harm by buying the field I saved you the bother of having a heathen neighbor who is like a "lion." Similarly, the law does not apply if the buyer is a heathen because the Jewish laws regarding fairness can only be imposed upon Jews. The "ban" mentioned here refers to the right of the Rabbis to punish a person who would not obey the law by forbidding other Jews to associate with him until he obeyed.

If a man sold a field in pledge to the man to whom it was pledged the law of first option does not apply. Rav Ashi said: The old men of Meta Meḥasya told me that the reason a pledge is called *mash-kanta* is because it *rests (shakhan)* with him who holds the pledge. For what purpose? For the law of first option.

In this case a field has been pledged to pay the debts of its owner. When the time for payment comes and the debtor cannot pay, the creditor can seize the field to get payment for his debt. If the debtor decided to sell the field to the creditor, the law of first option would not apply since the creditor has an earlier claim than the owner of the neighboring field. Rav Ashi was the head of the college at Sura on the Euphrates of which Meta Meḥasya was a twin city. The old men of this town had a pun on the word mashkanta. The creditor "dwells" with the field i.e. he has the first option.

If a man sells a field that is distant from his home in order to buy one nearer, or if he sells one that is poor in order to buy one that is good, the law of first option does not apply.

In the cases mentioned the law of first option does not apply because a sale of this nature is advantageous to the seller and he cannot be expected to give up his advantage.

The law of first option does not apply when a field is sold for the purpose of raising money to pay poll-tax or to support a widow or for a funeral. This is in keeping with what the scholars of Nehardea said, that in order to raise money for poll-tax or the support of a widow or for a funeral, an estate can be sold without public announcement.

When money is required urgently the law of first option does not apply because he needs the money right away and should be allowed to conclude the sale as soon as possible. The three cases are: to pay the tax the Persian government levied on every Jew, to pay out of an estate the cost of supporting the widow of the owner, and to pay for a funeral. When a debtor's goods were sold to pay his debt the Rabbis ruled that a public announcement of the sale should first be made so that people know about it and the best possible price would be obtainable. But the scholars of Nehardea exempted cases where a quick sale was required.

The law of first option does not apply if a man sold a field to a woman or to an orphan or to a partner.

In those days it was considered undignified for a woman to spend too much time doing business and hence a quick sale was advised. Consequently, when a field is sold to a woman the law of first option does not apply. The same applies to a field sold to an orphan because the protection and advancement of orphans comes before anything else. The reference to a partner means, according to the great commentator Rashi, that if two partners own the neighboring field any one of them can buy the field for sale even if the other does not know about it.

Where there are neighbors in the town and neighbors in the country the town neighbors come first; a neighbor and a scholar, the scholar

comes first; a relative and a scholar, the scholar comes first. They asked: What is the law regarding a neighbor and a relative? Come and hear: "Better is a neighbor that is near than a brother that is far off" (Proverbs 27:10).

Rashi argues that this paragraph does not refer to the normal case of first option but to the question of who shall have precedence when a field is for sale when the question of the neighboring field does not apply. A man should give the first option to his neighbors, but he should give preference to town neighbors rather than to neighbors in the country. The necessity for this choice could only arise of course if he had two homes or farms, one in the country and the other in town. The other details explain themselves.

The law of first option does not apply where one gives good coins and the other weighty coins.

In those days some coins were "good" i.e. were acceptable as currency in many parts but were not "weighty" i.e. did not have as much silver as "weighty" coins. Some merchants preferred "good" coins, others "weighty." Hence, if the buyer has "weighty" coins and the owner of the neighboring field "good" coins or vice versa, the seller can please himself as to which type of the two types of coin he would prefer and could, if necessary, disregard the law of first option which here could possibly be to his disadvantage.

The law of first option does not apply where one offers coins that are tied up in a package and the other coins that are not so bound.

Some merchants might be unwilling to accept coins tied up in a package out of fear that the man to whom they belong might claim that there were more coins in the package than it actually contained.

If the owner of the neighboring field said: "I will go and trouble myself to bring the money for the field," we do not wait for him. But if he simply said: "I will go and bring the money," then we must look into the matter. If he is a rich man who can easily bring the money we wait for him, otherwise we do not wait for him.

*Supposing the owner of the neighboring field is willing to buy
and pay for the field but asks the seller to wait until he fetches the
money, then it all depends. If he suggested that he has to go
to some trouble to raise the money the seller need not wait
because he is justified in fearing that he will not be able to
raise the money and, consequently, the sale will fall through. If
he simply asks for additional time to bring the money, it would
then depend upon whether he is the sort of person who would
have ready money available.*

**If land belongs to one man and the buildings on it to another, the
owner of the land can restrain the owner of the buildings, but the
owner of the buildings cannot restrain the owner of the land. If land
belongs to one man and the palm trees growing on it to another,
the owner of the land can restrain the owner of the palm trees but
the owner of the palm trees cannot restrain the owner of the land.**

*A wants to sell a field neighboring on the field belonging to B
and C has buildings on B's land. B has the first option on A's land
not C.*

**If there is an option of selling land for sowing and for building, the
provision of homes is more important so that the law of first option
does not apply in this case.**

*A has a field for sale. B, owner of the neighboring field, wishes
to buy it for sowing but C wishes to buy it for building homes.
The court has the first duty of seeing to it that homes are provided
for people and hence B in this case cannot legally claim the first
option.*

**If a stony ridge or a row of palm trees divided the two fields, then
it depends on the following. If the owner of the neighboring field
can approach the field to be sold even with one furrow the law of
first option applies, otherwise it does not apply.**

*If a stone ridge or a row of palms divide the two fields, are they
to be treated as neighboring fields? The answer is given that the
test is whether the plough can get through from one field to
the other.*

If a field was surrounded by the fields of four men and one of them bought it before the others the sale is valid. But if they all come together then it should be divided diagonally.

If four men all have the first option because they all own a neighboring field then it can be sold to the one who requests it first. However, if they all make the claim together the only thing to do is to sell the middle field to all four or rather a quarter of it to each of them so that each gets a triangle of land formed by the diagonals from the corner.

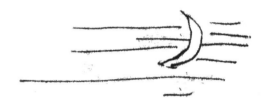

The Codes

WE HAVE SEEN in our earlier notes that eventually the Talmud became the source of authority in matters of Jewish law. But the Talmud is a very difficult work and only the most outstanding scholars were able to know it really well. Then again a law might not be found clearly stated in any one passage of the Talmud but one might have to search through many passages and put them together before the actual ruling could be arrived at. Moreover, Jews lived in different lands in which new conditions of life demanded decisions on questions not found at all in the Talmud. These were given by the great teachers from the time of the Geonim onward (6th century and later) but these decisions were frequently less available than the Talmud. Finally, it often happened that over the years more than one decision had come down from the past on the same question and it was hard for the ordinary scholar to know which should be followed.

As a result of all this, it became necessary from time to time for outstanding teachers of the law to compile collections or codes of Jewish law which would incorporate all the material which had accumulated to their day. Some of these codes only had a limited acceptance, but in the history of Jewish law there are three great Codes in particular which enjoyed the foremost authority. These are: 1) The *Yad Ha-Ḥazakah;* 2) The *Tur;* and 3) The *Shulḥan Arukh.* We proceed to describe each of these in turn.

MAIMONIDES' CODE OF LAW

Moses Maimonides (1135-1204) was undoubtedly the greatest Jew of the Middle Ages. In his middle years this famous teacher resolved to gather together all the earlier material of Jewish law and present it in orderly, logically organized form, written in clear, easy-to-read Hebrew. The gigantic task is said to have taken him about ten years. Not content with recording systematically all the laws which were in vogue in his day, he followed Rabbi Judah the Prince in setting down the whole range of law. So he treated laws appertaining to the Temple and its worship and other laws which were only of historical interest in his day.

Maimonides draws on all the earlier authorities so that most of the laws he records are already found in the earlier sources, particularly the Talmud. He decided to leave out the names of the various Rabbis whose views he records so that what we have is a kind of abstract statement of what the law is in any set of circumstances. His contribution was to give it all a logical shape and systematic presentation.

The resulting Code is in fourteen books, each of them divided into sections and each section sub-divided into the smaller units of chapters and "laws" i.e. individual laws. He called the work "Mishneh Torah," which means "Second to the Torah" i.e. this work was to take its place side by side with the Torah as the statement of what Judaism is about. However, Maimonides' very ambitious plan did not, in fact, win out. Subsequent teachers and even a number of contemporaries disagreed with his decisions so that the process of elaboration, elucidation and application continued. After Maimonides' death another name was given to the work. This was: *Yad Ha-Ḥazakah* (The Strong Hand). This title is an ingenious one. Maimonides' full name was Moses son of Maimon. Now in the book of Deuteronomy we read of the "strong hand" which Moses wrought (Deuteronomy 34:12). But the title is even more appropriate in that the Hebrew letters for "hand" are *yod* and *dalet* and, since every Hebrew letter is also a number, these total *fourteen,* the number of the "books" in the work. Maimonides is also known as the Rambam (Rabbi Moshe ben Maimon) and his work is frequently called too, the Rambam.

THE TUR

Maimonides' Code catered chiefly for the Jews of Spain and the countries under Spanish influence because Maimonides himself belonged to this background. There were, however, strong Jewish communities in other parts of Europe, in Germany and France for example, and these needed their own codifiers. The most famous of the German Codes was the *Tur* of Rabbi Jacob ben Asher.

Rabbi Jacob ben Asher died sometime before the year 1340, though we no longer know the exact year of his birth or death. His father Rabbi Asher was the most outstanding rabbinic figure in the Germany of his day. Rabbi Jacob's plan was to present Jewish law in four great books. Unlike Maimonides he codified only those laws in vogue in his day.

The word *Tur* means row (plural *Turim*). It is the word used in Scripture for the four rows of precious stones on the breastplate of the High Priest.

The four sections or books of the *Tur* (the four *Turim*) are:

1) *Oraḥ Ḥayyim:*   "The Way of Life" dealing with the daily rules of the Jew's life e.g. prayer and the festivals.

2) *Yoreh Deah:*   "Teaching of Knowledge" dealing with laws for more unusual circumstances and chiefly for the study of the experts e.g. how to write a Torah scroll.

3) *Even Ha-Ezer:*   "The Stone of Help" dealing with the laws of marriage and divorce.

4) *Ḥoshen Mishpat:*   "The Breastplate of Judgment" dealing with law proper, judges, damages and the like.

THE SHULḤAN ARUKH

The *Shulḥan Arukh*, "The Prepared Table," is the most important of all Codes of Jewish law and the one which became most authoritative.

Rabbi Joseph Karo, the author of the *Shulḥan Arukh,* was born in the year 1488 and died in the year 1575. In his day Jewish law was in a chaotic state. The earlier Codes were frequently in conflict. Different communities followed different rulings and it was not unusual for a Jewish traveler from place to place to find his religion and its laws receiving a different application in every place he visited. As Rabbi Joseph Karo remarks: There is not one Torah but many.

Rabbi Karo resolved to do something about this state of affairs. He first wrote a lengthy commentary to the *Tur,* in which he examined all the decisions of the earlier codifiers and tried to arrive at a fair consensus of opinion to be followed. His final decisions he recorded in the *Shulḥan Arukh,* hence its name i.e. the table arranged for eating. Rabbi Karo followed exactly the same arrangement as the *Tur.* The *Shulḥan Arukh* has the same four books with the same titles.

But for all his desire to be fair, Rabbi Karo tended generally to follow the Spanish authorities and this meant that his Code was insufficient for the great mass of Polish Jews (Poland in the sixteenth century was a great center of strong Jewish life and it was the German custom that was chiefly followed there). A solution might have been to have had a Polish *Shulḥan Arukh* but this would have made the differences between the two Jewries even more acute. The happy solution was found by the famous Rabbi of Cracow in Poland, Rabbi Moses Isserles (1510-1572). Rabbi Isserles added many notes to the text of the *Shulḥan Arukh* recording all the instances where the Polish and German custom differed from the Spanish as recorded by Rabbi Karo. Thus the reader of the *Shulḥan Arukh* was able to see at a glance where he stood in matters of law. If he noted that Rabbi Isserles had nothing to add to the decision of Rabbi Karo he knew that this decision was binding upon everyone. If, on the other hand, he saw a note in which Rabbi Isserles dissented, he knew that if he were to follow the Polish-German custom he should disregard Rabbi Karo's ruling and follow Rabbi Isserles. Rabbi Isserles called his notes the *Mappah,* "The Tablecloth" i.e. to the "Table" of Rabbi Karo.

Although Jewish law did not stand still after the *Shulḥan Arukh,* it became the most authoritative Code of Jewish law right down to the present day. Perhaps the main reason for this is that it was the first great Code to be compiled after the invention of printing and hence produced in many more thousands of copies than could have been possible for any of the earlier codes.

Many distinguished Rabbis wrote commentaries to the *Shulḥan Arukh*. Some of them published abridgements of it for more popular use. Our final example in this section is of one such abridgement published in the last century.

The Jewish lawyers and teachers who flourished before the period of the *Shulḥan Arukh* are now known in the literature of Jewish law as the *Rishonim*, "the early ones," whereas the scholars who flourished after the *Shulḥan Arukh* are known as the *Aḥaronim*, "the later ones." Generally speaking the *Rishonim* are held to be greater experts and enjoy a far greater reputation than the *Aḥaronim* so that a later Rabbi in his attempt to decide a knotty problem in law will do his best to substantiate his case by referring to rulings of the *Rishonim*.

CHAPTER 19

MAIMONIDES' YAD HA-HAZAKAH,
HILKHOT GEZELAH VA-AVEDAH, CHAPTER 1

On robbery and covetousness

The different kinds of robbery and their punishment.

Whoever robs his neighbor or anything worth a *perutah* **offends against a negative command, as it is said: "Thou shalt not rob him" (Leviticus 19:13). But he is not flogged for this crime since Scripture provides him with a positive command, namely, that if he has robbed, he must return it, as it is said: "He shall restore that which he took by robbery" (Leviticus 5:23). This is a positive command. He is not flogged even if he has burnt that which he took by robbery since he is obliged to pay for it and there is no punishment of flogging for a negative command for which there is repayment.**

A perutah is a small coin, the smallest coin of the realm in Talmudic times. A negative command is a command in Scripture of the form: "Thou shalt not . . ." as opposed to a positive command which is a command to do something. In the scheme of the Rabbis an offense against a negative command could carry with it the penalty of flogging administered by the court. However, when Scripture provides an alternative in the form of a positive command, by which the wrong can be righted, there is no flogging. Hence Maimonides says that there is no flogging for robbery because it can be put right either by restoring the actual object stolen or by giving back its value.

According to the Torah it is forbidden to rob anyone of even the smallest amount. It is forbidden to rob or to oppress even a non-Jew and if he did rob from him or oppress him he is obliged to give back that which he has taken.

Maimonides means here that although the full offense is only incurred when the amount stolen is at least of the value of a perutah, it is still forbidden to steal even the smallest amount. Naturally there is no difference whether the victim is a Jew or a non-Jew.

What is meant by "robbing"? This is when he takes someone's money by force; where, for example he snatched some object from his hands or where he entered the domain of another without permission and removed from there some vessels, or where he took hold of his slave or his animal and put them to work for himself, or where he went into his neighbor's field and ate the fruit growing there. All such instances are cases of robbery, as it is said: "And robbed the spear out of the hand of the Egyptian" (II Samuel 23:21).

The significance of this paragraph is that the Talmud draws a distinction between "theft" (genevah) and "robbery" (gezelah). The latter dealt with here is open theft, the former stealing by stealth i.e. at night when no one is about and when the victim does not know who has done it. According to the Rabbis the former was a worse offense than the latter, hence the Torah orders the thief to pay double the amount stolen if he is found out whereas the robber only has to pay the amount stolen. The verse quoted is for the purpose of demonstrating that the term "robbing" applies to direct stealing, not by stealth.

What is meant by "oppression"? This refers to where some money of his neighbor came into his possession with the consent of its owner but when the owner claims it he keeps it by force and refuses to return it. If, for instance, he owed money to his neighbor who had loaned it to him or he had hired something from his neighbor and had not yet paid for it and his neighbor claims the money but cannot get it back from him because he is powerful and hard. It is with regard to this that Scripture says: "Thou shalt not oppress thy neighbor" (Leviticus 19:13).

*"Oppression" in the verse is said here to have a rather limited
meaning i.e. when the robber keeps for himself something which
belongs to his neighbor. In both "robbery" and "oppression"
(unlike "theft") the victim knows who is guilty. The difference
between them is that in the case of robbery there was a direct action
whereas in the case of oppression the property was obtained in
the first instance in a legitimate way i.e. by loan. "Powerful and
hard" means that the robber is too strong to be forced by the
courts to yield his illgotten gains.*

**Whoever is guilty of robbery must return the very thing he had
robbed, as it is said: "He shall restore that which he took by robbery"
(Leviticus 5:23). If the object he had taken by robbery had been lost
or had been changed into something else he is obliged to pay its
value. Whether he confessed to the robbery or whether witnesses
testify that he is guilty he is only obliged to pay the actual amount.
The law of the Torah is that even if he robbed another of a beam
which he built into his house, since the beam has undergone no
change, he is obliged to take the whole house to pieces in order to
restore the beam to its rightful owner. However, the Rabbis, in order
to encourage robbers to repent, arranged that in such a case he can
restore the value of the beam and not be obliged to destroy the
whole house. The same law applies to all such cases. Even with
regard to someone who robbed his neighbor of a beam, which he
then used to build a tabernacle on the festival of Tabernacles, he is
obliged to restore only the value of the beam, if the owner claimed it
during the festival. But if he claimed it after the festival he must
restore the beam itself since it had not been changed and had not
been fixed with mortar.**

*The robber cannot offer simply to pay the value of the object
he has stolen. He must give back the thing itself. However, if this
is no longer possible i.e. when the object has been lost or changed
into something else (cloth, for example, that has been cut up and
made into a garment) he is obliged to restore its value. But, as
stated earlier, he is not obliged to pay more than the value i.e.
unlike a "thief" who has to pay double. (Even the thief only
has to pay double if he is found out, not if he confesses, hence the
wording of the rule in this paragraph.) Although the original rule
of the Torah demands that the man who built the beam into*

his house is obliged to destroy the house in order to return the beam, the Rabbis, knowing that this would prevent the robber from repenting, encouraged him by accepting his right to pay only the value. This is an interesting example of how the Rabbis were more concerned with the improvement of society than with punishing the criminal. The tabernacle is only for use for the seven days of the festival, hence after the festival he can be expected to demolish it in order to restore the beam.

If a man robs someone else of something worth less than a *perutah,* **even though he has sinned, he is not obliged to restore it to him. Supposing someone robbed another of three bundles of vegetables worth three** *perutot* **and afterwards the price went down so that they were only worth two** *perutot* **and he gave back to him only two of them, then he is obliged to give back the third one, too, since it was worth a** *perutah* **at the time of the robbery. If he robbed him of two bundles worth a** *perutah* **and gave back only one he is no longer guilty of the crime of robbery but he has not carried out the duty of restoring that which he had robbed.**

The point here is that a "restoration" of less than a perutah is too small to be called "restoration." In the last case the robber is no longer guilty of "robbery" since, having restored one of the bundles, he no longer is a robber of property to the value of a perutah, but he now cannot carry out the duty of restoration since what he has retained is not worth a perutah.

If a man robs his neighbor of something in an inhabited place and wishes to restore it in the desert, then the law is that the victim can please himself. If he wants to take it back in the desert he can do so but if he wishes he can say: I will only take it back in an inhabited place because in the desert it might be taken from me by force. In the latter case it would remain in the possession of the robber and he would be responsible for it until he gives it back to him in an inhabited place. The same rule applies to the return of the value of that which he had taken by robbery.

If something was stolen from a man in the desert it can be returned in the desert. But not in the case mentioned because the restoration must be in the same circumstances as the robbery i.e.

*where there is the same risk to the owner. In the desert there is
far greater risk of having the thing stolen by force than in the town.*

If a man robbed his neighbor of some money and then returned it
to him by adding it to some other account to be paid to him, he
has carried out the duty of returning that which he had robbed. If he
put the money in the victim's money-bag he has carried out his
duty. For since it is usual for a man to count his money from time to
time he will have counted the money returned to him together with
the rest of his money and such an indirect counting is enough to
exempt the robber. But if the robber put the money in a bag which
did not contain money he has not carried out his duty and is still
responsible for the money he has robbed until he informs the victim
that he has put it in such-and-such a bag.

*In this case the robber wishes to return that which he has stolen
but is ashamed to do so. Consequently, he takes the opportunity
of slipping the money to the victim by paying him more when
paying another debt or when buying from him. But such restoration
must be of a nature that will bring it to the attention of the
victim pretty soon, otherwise the robber is still responsible for
repayment if someone else stole it from the victim or if the victim
lost it.*

Whoever covets his neighbor's slave or maidservant or his house
or his vessels or anything else he can buy from him and exercises
every kind of persuasion until he obtains that which he covets,
offends against a negative command, even if he gives him much
money, as it is said: "Thou shalt not covet" (Exodus 20:14). There is
no penalty of flogging for this negative command since no action
is involved. He does not offend against this negative command until
he actually takes the object he coveted, as it is said: "Thou shalt not
covet the silver or the gold that is on them and take it unto thee"
(Deuteronomy 7:25)—coveting that involves action.

*Maimonides here states that the tenth commandment: "Thou shalt
not covet" is also expressed in Scripture by the words: "Thou shalt
not desire." These expressions refer to different offenses. "To desire"
something belonging to someone else is, according to this rule, to
plan how to get hold of it (even if the plan includes eventual
payment for it). "To covet" is to go beyond the planning stage and*

actually obtain it for oneself even though the owner does not really wish to sell it. (If he wishes to sell then, of course, it is a simple business transaction.) The penalty of flogging is only for a negative command which involves an action, not here. It might be argued that this, too, involves an action since he only offends if he actually acquires it but Maimonides' point is that the action (of buying the object) is not wrong in itself. It is the coveting which is wrong and this involves no action. The verse is quoted to demonstrate that the term "to covet" involves an action of some kind. It follows from all this that the tenth commandment does not mean that if a man sees something belonging to another he may not say to himself: "I wish I had one of those" but only to the man who plans to get the thing coveted. If, for instance, a man sees that his friend has a Rolls Royce car it is not forbidden for him to say to himself: "I wish I had a Rolls Royce." What is forbidden is for him to plan how he can get this particular Rolls Royce, even though he knows that the owner does not really wish to sell it. Once he begins to think along these lines he has offended against: "Thou shalt not desire" and once his plans have materialized and he has obtained the car he offends against: "Thou shalt not covet."

Whoever desires his neighbor's house or his wife or his vessels or any such things as he can buy from him, then no sooner than he thinks to himself how to acquire this thing and no sooner does he set his mind to getting it than he offends against a negative command, as it is said: "Thou shalt not desire" (Deuteronomy 5:18). "Desire" is in the heart alone.

The paragraph is explained in the previous note.

Desiring another's property leads to coveting it and this in turn leads to robbery since if the owner does not want to sell even after much persuasion he will come to rob from him, as it is said: "And they covet fields and take them by violence" (Micah 2:2). If the owner stands up to him in order to save his property or to prevent it being stolen it can lead to murder. Go and consider the story of Ahab and Naboth.

Maimonides states that the reason why "desiring" and "coveting" are forbidden is that they tempt a man to steal that which he wants so badly if he cannot get it otherwise and they might even lead eventually to murder. The story of Ahab and Naboth is to be found in the first book of Kings, chapter 21.

It follows from the above that anyone who desires the property of another offends against one negative command and anyone who actually acquires the object he desired through much persuasion or begging offends against two negative commands. Therefore Scripture says: "Thou shalt not covet" and "Thou shalt not desire." If he actually steals he offends against three negative commands.

Each step in the process involves a further transgression, from "desiring" to "coveting" to "stealing."

Whoever robs his neighbor of anything worth a *perutah* it is as if he had taken his life from him, as it is said: "So are the ways of every one that is greedy of gain; who taketh away the life of the owners thereof" (Proverbs 1:19). Nevertheless the Rabbis ordained that if the object stolen was no longer in existence and the robber who wished to repent came of his own accord and wished to return the value of the thing stolen, it should not be accepted. But the robber should be helped and forgiven in order to bring the upright way near to those who repent. Whoever accepts from the robber the value of the thing stolen, the spirit of the sages is displeased with such a person.

The saying that to take something of another is like taking his life is, of course, an exaggeration yet it expresses the truth that when something belonging to another is taken from him something of the person himself is taken away. Maimonides first says this in order that the reader should not imagine, from what comes later, that robbery is to be treated as a light matter. It is a very serious offense, yet for all that, every effort should be made to encourage the thief to repent. If every victim of a robber insisted that the robber should return the value of the stolen goods this would effectively prevent robbers ever giving up their evil ways. For they would argue that repentance would involve them in giving away all that they have. The Rabbis tell of a well-known robber who was sorry for his evil life and wished to turn over a new leaf. But his wife said to him: Fool! If you do that the very sash you wear will no longer be your own. Here again we find the Rabbis more interested in improving society than in punishing the criminal.

On almsgiving

The laws of correct and incorrect methods
of giving and taking charity.

We must be more careful in carrying out our charitable obligations than we are with regard to all the other positive commands of the Torah, since charity is the distinguishing mark of the righteous man, the descendant of Abraham our father. As it is said: "For I have singled him out, that he may instruct his children and his descendants to keep the way of the Lord by practicing charity" (Genesis 18:19). Furthermore, Israel's throne is only established and the true religion only made to survive through charity, as it is said: "With charity shalt thou be established" (Isaiah 54:14). And Israel is only redeemed because of the charity which Israel practices, as it is said: "Zion shall be redeemed with judgment, and those who return to her with charity" (Isaiah 1:27).

A "positive precept" is a command in Scripture for something to be done as opposed to a "negative precept," a command not to do something. "Love thy neighbor," for example, is a positive precept; "Thou shalt not steal" is a negative precept. The Hebrew word for "righteous man" is "tzaddik" which has the same root as the word for charity, "tzedakah." The saying about the true religion surviving probably means that there can be no future to a religion unless it teaches kindliness and compassion. Man cannot hold fast to a cruel, unfeeling religion. It is interesting that Maimonides, following the Rabbis of the Talmud, holds that a Jew is known as a Jew because he is kind. This is his distinguishing mark.

No man ever becomes poor through giving charity and neither evil nor harm ever results from charity, as it is said: "And the work of charity shall be peace" (Isaiah 32:17). Whoever is merciful will be treated mercifully, as it is said: "And He will give you compassion and show you compassion and increase you" (Deuteronomy 13:18). The ancestry of anyone who is cruel-hearted and lacks compassion is suspect, for cruelty is only to be found among the heathen, as it is said: "They are cruel and will not show mercy" (Jeremiah 50:42). All Israelites and those who join the ranks of Israel are like brothers, as it is said: "Ye are children of the Lord your God" (Deuteronomy 14:1) and who else will have mercy if brother has no mercy on brother? To whom can the poor of Israel turn their eyes—can it be to the heathen who hate them and persecute them? Their eyes turn only to their brothers.

The usual excuse for refusing to help others is the fear that by giving away some of one's wealth one might become poor oneself. Maimonides here says that this is only an excuse because people do not, in fact, become poor through giving charity. Of course some prudence must be exercised. Elsewhere the Rabbis teach that it is wrong to give away more than a fifth of one's income. The final remarks in this paragraph have to be understood against their historical background. Maimonides lived in an age when Jews were frequently persecuted for their religion and they could hardly expect non-Jews to be of any help to them if their fellow-Jews would not. Even in modern times Jewish communities have taken pride in organizing their own charities rather than have their co-religionists supported by general charities.

Whoever turns his eyes away from charity is called a "scoundrel" just as idolators are called "scoundrels." With regard to idolatry it is said: "Some scoundrels from among you have gone" (Deuteronomy 13:14), and with regard to one who turns his eyes away from charity it is said: "Beware that there be not the thought of a scoundrel in thy heart" (Deuteronomy 15:9). Such a person is also called "wicked," as it is said: "The tender mercies of the wicked are cruel" (Proverbs 12:10). And he is called a sinner," as it is said: "And he cry unto the Lord against thee, and it is a sin unto thee" (Deuteronomy 15:9). The Holy One, blessed be He, is near to the cry of the poor, as it is said: "Thou hearest the cry of the poor." It is therefore essential never to cause the poor to cry out in pain for God has made them a promise, as it is said: "And it shall come to pass when he crieth unto Me, that I will hear; for I am gracious" (Exodus 22:27).

The point Maimonides makes in this paragraph is that although a failure to give charity is a failure to carry out a duty, not a definite sin, it is nonetheless treated as if it were a sin. Hence Maimonides says that the man who intentionally disregards the claims of the poor is called by Scripture a "scoundrel" etc. Maimonides quotes as a Scriptural verse: "Thou hearest the cry of the poor." In fact, there is no such verse. Maimonides quoting from memory has probably confused it with the verse: "He will hear the cry of the poor" (Job 34:28).

Whoever gives alms to a poor man but gives with an evil look on his face and with his face stuck in the ground loses and destroys any merit he would otherwise have had, even if he gave him a thousand zuz. Rather he should give him with a cheerful face and with joy and share the poor man's anguish with him, as it is said: "Did I not weep for him that was in trouble? Was not my soul grieved for the poor?" (Job 30:25). And he should speak to him words of comfort and consolation, as it is said: "And I caused the widow's heart to sing for joy" (Job 29:13).

The expression "his face stuck in the ground" is idiomatic. The meaning is that he behaves as if he could not bear to look the poor man in the face and has utter contempt for him. A thousand zuz was a very large sum of money. A small house could have been bought in Talmudic times for two hundred zuz. In the famous Passover hymn a kid is bought for two zuz. When a man gives cheerfully to the poor there is less feeling of inadequacy on the part of the recipient.

If a poor man asks you for alms and you have nothing to give him then appease him by speaking kindly to him. It is forbidden to upbraid a poor man or to raise one's voice to him because his heart is crushed and broken and it is said: "A broken and crushed heart, O God, Thou wilt not despise" (Psalms 51:19). And it says further: "To revive the spirit of the humble, and to revive the heart of the contrite ones" (Isaiah 57:15). Woe to anyone who puts a poor man to shame. Woe to him. But he should be as a father to the poor both in speech and in compassion, as it is said, "I was a father to the poor" (Job 29:16).

It is perhaps natural that when a man has nothing to give the poor he should feel guilty and be tempted to vent his spleen on the poor man. Maimonides here says that he should resist the temptation. He should make up for his inability to help by giving the poor man some words of encouragement. The secret is, says Maimonides, to behave as if he were the poor man's father who has complete compassion for his needy son.

One who compels others to give charity and raises money for charitable causes has a greater reward than the givers themselves, as it is said: "And the work of charity shall be peace" (Isaiah 32:17). It is with reference to people like charity collectors that it is said: "And they that turn many to righteousness will be as the stars for ever and ever" (Daniel 12:3).

Some people are quite prepared to give to charity themselves but cannot bear to ask others to give. This is too embarrassing for them and too much bother. But a community needs its keen charity workers prepared to collect money and distribute it fairly. Consequently, the collectors and administrators are in many ways more important than the actual givers. This is particularly so since they have to act as go-betweens and face the annoyance of both the givers and the poor themselves who may not be satisfied with the amount distributed to them. The verse from Scripture speaks of the work of charity which is here interpreted to mean the task of persuading others to give.

There are eight degrees of charity, one higher than the other. The highest degree of all is where one strengthens the hands of an Israelite who faces poverty, giving him a gift or a loan or entering into a business partnership with him or giving him a job in order to strengthen his hand and so prevent him becoming an object of charity. It is with regard to this that Scripture says: "Then thou shalt strengthen him: Yea, though he be a stranger, or a sojourner; that he may live with thee" (Leviticus 25:35). The meaning is, strengthen him before he falls and needs to be supported by others.

Maimonides now records his famous eight degrees of charity. The highest is so to help a man in financial trouble that disaster is avoided and his need for charity negated. Maimonides records various ways of providing this kind of help. He may give him some money to tide him over the difficult patch or better still offer him a loan of money to be repaid when better times come. Or he can take him into partnership in his own business or get him a job so as to save his self-respect.

A lesser degree is when one gives charity to the poor but neither the giver nor the receiver knows of the other. For in this case the duty of giving charity for its own sake has been carried out. In the Temple, for example, there was a secret chamber into which good men would secretly place money and from which the poor would take secretly. Not very different from this is where a man gives money to the charity chest. But a man should only give money into a charity chest if he knows that the directors are trustworthy, wise and reliable like Rabbi Ḥananya son of Teradyon.

The next degree is where charity is given to those already poor but without either the giver or the receiver knowing of one another. In this case the poor man is not put to shame and the giver cannot face him in a superior fashion as his benefactor. Hence this is an example of a good deed performed for its own sake not simply to win the esteem of others. The Talmud states that in the Temple there was a secret room for the purpose mentioned by Maimonides. A man should only donate money to a charitable cause, says Maimonides, if he can rely on the administrators to be fair and reliable and not squander the money with which they have been trusted or, worse, use it for themselves. The classic example of a reliable charity administrator was Rabbi Ḥananya son of Teradyon (second century). The Talmud says that once Rabbi Ḥananya had a large sum of money in his house which he had collected for charity. When this was stolen from his home he made it up out of his own pocket rather than let the charity suffer.

A lesser degree is where the giver knows to whom he has given but the poor man does not know to whom he is indebted. The famous sages, for example, would go in secret to throw some money into the houses of the poor. This is the desirable way of giving charity when the directors of the charity chest are unreliable.

In this case the benefactor knows whom he is benefitting but the poor man does not know to whom he is indebted. Although this degree is lower than the previous one Maimonides thinks that it should be preferred whenever there are doubts as to the reliability of the charity administrators.

Less than this is where the poor man knows to whom he is indebted but the giver does not know to whom he has given. Some of the famous sages would wrap their contributions for charity in a scarf slung over their shoulder so that the poor could come and take it without suffering embarrassment.

In this case the poor man knows to whom he is indebted but the benefactor does not know whom he has benefitted and, moreover, the poor man knows that he does not know.

Less than this is when the giver gives money directly to the poor man but without having to be asked for it.

This degree is where the money is given directly so that both giver and receiver know one another's identity but instead of waiting for the poor man to beg the giver generously gives before he is asked to do so.

Less than this is when he gives after the poor man has asked him to do so.

Here he gives, but only when asked to do so.

Less than this is when he gives the poor man less than he should but with a cheerful countenance.

This is still a lower degree. He does give, but not as much as he ought to. However, no matter how little he gives he does give cheerfully.

Less than this is when the giver is glum.

The lowest of all is where he gives grudgingly and with an unpleasant manner.

The great Sages used to give a small coin to the poor before every prayer and only then would they pray, as it is said: "As for me, I will behold Thy face in righteousness" (Psalms 17:15).

When a man prays he casts himself on God's mercy but how can he have the cheek to do this unless he himself is merciful to others? Hence some of the wise men of old (this is a name for the sages of the Talmud) would give at least a small coin to charity before beginning their prayers.

If a father supports his grown-up sons and daughters, whom he has no legal obligation to support, in order that the sons should study the Torah and the daughters be trained to lead a good life and not suffer degradation, and so, too, a son who supports his parents, all these belong to the practice of charity and are, in fact, a superior form of charity, for near relations have priority in charity matters. Whoever has the poor and orphans as guests at his table God will answer when he calls on Him and he will find delight, as it is said: "Then thou shalt call and the Lord will answer" (Isaiah 58:9).

According to Jewish law there is no obligation for a father to support his children once they are grown-up, but if he does so it is an act of charity and is to be preferred to giving to strangers. Some people might disagree with this but in the Rabbinic view there is something "phoney" about a man who cares for others but neglects his own family. The reference to the poor and the orphan is based on the Rabbinic teaching that widows and orphans should be treated with special consideration, even if they are rich.

The Sages advise a man to have the poor and the orphan as servants in his household instead of having slaves to do the work. It is better that he be served by these, so that the descendants of Abraham, Isaac and Jacob benefit from his wealth, rather than the descendants of Ham. For whoever adds slaves to his household causes day by day sin and iniquity to increase in the world. But if the poor are members of his household he increases merit and good deeds all the time.

Slavery had not yet been abolished by Maimonides' day and Jews were permitted to own slaves. In a good household slaves were fairly well-treated and had quite a good time. But there was a general belief that slaves were prone to theft and other kinds of immorality. Hence Maimonides says that it is far better to employ needy people to work in the household instead of buying slaves to do the work. The reference to Ham is based on the story in the book of Genesis (Genesis 9:27) that Noah's son Ham was cursed that his descendant's should be slaves.

A man should force himself to suffer anguish rather than have his needs satisfied by others and cast himself on the mercy of the community. And so did the Sages advise: "Make thy Sabbath as a week-day rather than be supported by others." Even if a man is an honored sage but poor, he should take a job, even if the work is unpleasant, rather than allow himself to be supported by others. It is better for a man to skin animal carcasses rather than say to the community: "Support me, I am a great sage, I am a priest." So did the Sages advise. Some of our greatest sages were woodcutters, log-carriers, water-drawers, iron-workers and smiths. They asked nothing of the community and refused to accept anything when it was offered.

Maimonides here says that a man should do his utmost to avoid taking charity. In the words of the Talmudic Rabbis, he should treat the Sabbath as a week-day rather than be supported by others. The Rabbis did not mean that a man should work on the Sabbath but that he should be prepared to give up for a time the special Sabbath foods and be satisfied with his normal week-day fare even on the Sabbath until he can afford something better. Self-respect demands that a person be content with frugal meals and less comfort and be independent of others rather than enjoy hearty meals and luxuries and be dependent for them on others.

Maimonides' reference to the Talmudic Sages is worthy of note. The Rabbi as a professional devoting all his time to his job and being paid for it was unknown until the 13th century. Maimonides himself, like many a Jewish teacher of his age, earned his living as a physician. But eventually it was realized that in the more complicated conditions of life the role of Rabbi is full-time and demanding so that it is quite in order for a community to pay its Rabbi an adequate salary without the Rabbi going counter to Maimonides' teaching here.

Whoever has no need to take charity but fools the people into believing that he is poor and takes will not die of old age until he is really obliged to be supported by others. Such a person is spoken of in the verse: "Cursed be the man who trusteth in men" (Jeremiah

17:5). Whoever needs to take charity and is unable to survive unless he takes, an old or sick person, for example, or a sufferer, and yet is too proud to take, such a person sheds blood and is responsible for adopting a suicidal attitude and has nothing but sin and guilt for his pains. But whoever needs to take but torments himself and disregards his situation in order to lead a life of suffering rather than bother the community, such a person will not die of old age until he has the privilege of supporting others. It is of such a person that the verse says: "Blessed is the man who trusteth in the Lord" (Jeremiah 17:7).

In those days, as in ours, there were people of means, who, instead of earning a living honestly, pretended to be poor so that they could live on charity. Maimonides says that the punishment of such a person is that eventually he will be forced to live on charity. Conversely, if a man puts his life in danger rather than take charity he is not to be admired but is guilty of having suicidal tendencies. When a man's circumstances are such that he has to rely on others to survive, he should be big enough to accept charity gracefully and not be too proud to do so. However, if a man feels that to live independently will not harm his health but only interfere with his comfort he is advised not to rely on charity and God will help him.

On judges and communal responsibility

The laws of correct conduct for a judge.

An unworthy judge should never be appointed. Whoever has a hand in appointing an unworthy judge, one who is unlearned in the Torah, even if he has other good qualities, offends against a negative precept of the Torah. The Sages say that whoever appoints an unworthy judge has done the equivalent of erecting a pillar for idolatry. Or it is as if he planted a grove for idolatry if he appoints him in a place where there are scholars. Furthermore the Sages expounded the verse: "Ye shall not make with Me gods of silver . . ." (Exodus 20:20) as referring to one who "comes by virtue of his silver and gold," namely, a judge appointed for his wealth.

The negative precept referred to here is: "Ye shall not respect persons in judgment" (Deuteronomy 1:17) which, according to the Rabbis, means, among other things, that a judge should not be appointed simply because he is popular if he is unfit to act as a judge i.e. because he is insufficiently familiar with the law. It was forbidden to "set up a pillar" i.e. as a token of worship, because of the idolatry of this form of worship, and it was forbidden to plant a sacred grove of trees, another type of idolatry. To appoint an unworthy judge was said to be a similar offense, perhaps because the person is "worshipped" instead of God i.e. he is placed before God and God's demands that justice be practiced. "In the place of scholars" means where there are learned men capable of doing the job. It appears that in those days unworthy men would sometimes buy themselves into office by offering gifts and the like to those who appointed them, hence the stern condemnation of those who appoint a judge simply because he is wealthy.

It is forbidden to have one's case tried by any judge appointed by virtue of his wealth. Not only this, but it is a religious duty to treat him with disdain and to insult him.

To emphasize how wrong it was to appoint a judge merely because of his wealth it was said that anyone who treated such a person lightly and disdained him was carrying out a religious duty. If the people do not accept such appointments, they will not be made.

But with regard to every worthy court of law in Israel the Divine Presence is with them. It is therefore necessary for judges to sit in fear and dread, properly dressed and with reverence.

God is with the judges when they decide correctly. Consequently when they sit in court they should sit as if they were, in a very special sense, in God's presence i.e. as if they were in Synagogue, for example. The reference to "proper dress" really means that, as was the practice in ancient times, the judges should wear special robes in order to impress the people with the dignity of their office.

It is forbidden for them to behave frivolously and to sit gossiping in the courthouse, but their conversation there should only be on matters of Torah and wisdom.

The judges cannot expect ordinary people to have respect for them if they have no respect themselves for their office.

The judge should see himself as if a sword were on his neck and as if Hell were open at his feet and he should know whom he is judging and before whom he is judging and who will punish him in the future if he departs from the strict line of justice, as it is said: "God stands in the assembly of the mighty, He judges in the midst of the judges" (Psalms 82:1). And it is further said: "Take heed what ye do; for ye judge not for man, but for the Lord, who is with you in the judgment" (II Chronicles 19:6).

The judge, in order to increase his sense of responsibility, should imagine that a sharp sword is at his neck and that if he gives an unjust decision it will slay him. Similarly he should imagine that Hell is open beneath his feet so that he will drop into Hell as soon as he renders an unjust decision. (The belief in Hell was very strong among the Rabbis. Many Jewish teachers, however, preferred to think of Hell not as an actual place but as the miserable state of mind of the sinner remote from God.) Do you remember the story of the sword of Damocles? The judge should further reflect on whom he is judging (that his decisions affect human lives), and before whom (that he is in the presence of God).

Any judge who does not give absolutely true decisions causes the Divine Presence to depart from Israel and any judge who unlawfully takes money from one person and gives it to another will be punished in his person by God.

The reference to punishment in person means that whereas the false judge has only caused someone an unjust financial loss, God will not be content that in retribution he should suffer merely a financial loss but he will be punished in his person by God.

But whenever a judge renders absolutely true decisions, even in one hour, it is as if he had put right the whole world and he causes the Divine Presence to rest upon Israel. If a judge says: "Why should I let myself in for this trouble?" Scripture says: "who is with you in the judgment" (II Chronicles 19:6): a judge is only expected to act upon that which his eyes see.

Without justice human society perishes. Consequently every true judge makes a contribution to human welfare and it is accounted as if he had "put right" the whole world. Since the judge's responsibility is terribly heavy a man may say, very well then I will never act as a judge, even if there is no one else to do the job. Why should I take the risk? To this the reply is given that all that is demanded of the judge is to be fair: he is not expected to be superhuman. If he makes a mistake through no fault of his own he is not to blame. God is with the judge in his judgments, which means that all that is expected of the judge is for him to decide as fairly as he can and leave the rest to God. In the words of the Rabbis he is only expected to notice that which his eyes see.

Maimonides writes: "It was the way of the early sages to run away from being appointed to high office and they would try their utmost to avoid being appointed as judges unless they knew that there were no others as efficient as they were so that if they refused to be appointed justice would suffer. And yet, even then, they would not act as judges until the people forced them into so acting and until the elders pleaded with them so to do." These are his words.

Maimonides is quoted to the effect that a man, even if he is worthy, should not run after high office but should only accept it if people plead with him to do so. Plato similarly says that the best leader is the person who does not want to be a leader.

It is forbidden for a judge to conduct himself with pride and an overbearing attitude to the community but only with humility and with respect.

The temptations of a man occupying a high office to behave with contempt for others is to be discouraged. Lord Acton once said that all power corrupts, absolute power corrupts absolutely. It is against the corruptions of power that these paragraphs are directed.

Any communal leader who acts autocratically out of ulterior motives will never have a scholarly son. And it is also forbidden to despise the members of the community even if they are ignoramuses.

The meaning of the reference to the scholarly son appears to be that God will punish him in this way. But it may also mean that if the son observes his father behaving in a haughty manner he will find no encouragement to engage himself in scholarship. He will argue if this is what learning has done to my father I had better keep away from it.

He should not tread on the heads of the holy people for even if they are ordinary folk and of low degree they are still the children of Abraham, Isaac and Jacob.

A judge tends to become self-righteous. As a warning against treating ordinary folk disrespectfully he is reminded that they had great ancestors. Chaim Weizmann once said that Jews are sometimes accused of being the sons of old clothes men. But, said Weizmann, if we are the sons of old clothes men, we are the grandsons of prophets. The expression "treading on the heads of the holy people" is idiomatic for a haughty attitude. It may have originated in the days when students sat on the ground in the college in ancient Palestine while the teachers stood over them.

It is necessary for him to bear the troubles of the community and their burden. As the Rabbis comment on the verse: "And gave them a charge unto the children of Israel" (Exodus 6:13)—"even if they curse you and throw stones at you."

A man in high office can frequently expect brickbats but he must be prepared to "take it." The Rabbis say that when God ordered Moses and Aaron to lead the people He warned them that they must be prepared to do this even if the people curse them and throw stones at them which, incidentally, did eventually happen, according to Scripture.

Just as the judge is obliged to behave correctly so, too, the community is obliged to have respect for the judge and to honor him.

The judge has obligations to the community but the community has its own obligations to the judge.

He, too, should not conduct himself in a disrespectful manner or behave frivolously in their presence.

Again the judge is warned that however small he is in his own eyes he must preserve the dignity of his office.

For once a man has been appointed to high office in the community it is forbidden for him to do any work in the presence of three people so as not to be treated disdainfully by them. It is, by an argument from the lesser to the great, forbidden for him to eat, drink and be merry in public and frequent assemblies of the ignorant since he is even forbidden to do work in public. Woe to the judges who do these things. They trespass against the Torah of Moses our teacher for they despise its laws and cast it down to the ground and make it reach the dust and they bring evil to themselves and their children both in this world and the next.

"Work" here means the kind of thing that men of dignity would not normally do.

It is also forbidden to show disrespect to the agent of the court. The court has a right to flog anyone who causes pain to the agent of the court in the exercise of his duties. The agent has the force of two witnesses in testifying against anyone who insults him and that person may then be placed under a ban.

The "agent of the court" was the ancient equivalent of the police officer. The methods of dealing with people who interfere with such officials was either to have them flogged or to place them under a ban. The man placed under a ban was in an unfortunate position. No one was allowed to talk to him or even to come near him until the ban had been lifted. These methods strike us as pretty drastic and, in fact, they eventually were discontinued in Jewish courts. However, we can understand the principle behind them. Unless there is respect for the law and the officers whose job it is to enforce it, justice dies. Compare this with the modern offense of "contempt of court."

The dignity befitting a Synagogue

The laws of treating a Synagogue with respect.

Jewish communities in the Middle Ages were generally small. Most Jews lived around the Synagogue or very near to it so that they had greater access to the Synagogue than we normally have and tended to treat it with greater familiarity than we do. The Synagogue proper was for prayer. Attached to the Synagogue, or near to it, there was generally to be found a special "House of Study" (Bet Ha-Midrash). Here, as the name implies, the Torah would be studied whenever people could take time off from their work. A "House of Study" was lined with volumes of sacred literature. Some scholars would spend most of their time engrossed in this literature and would even eat and sleep in the "House of Study" so as not to waste any of their precious time.

Rabbi Moses Isserles' notes on Karo's text appear in brackets.

One should not behave in a frivolous manner in a Synagogue or a House of Study, to crack jokes there, for example, or indulge in humorous or pointless conversation. One should not eat or drink there nor should one adorn oneself there or walk around there. One should not enter there in summer to cool off or in winter to seek shelter from the rain. In an emergency scholars and their pupils are permitted to eat and drink there. [Some say that in a House of Study

this is permitted even where there is no emergency.] No monetary calculations should be made there unless they are for religious purposes, collecting money for charity, for example, or for the release of captives. No funeral orations should be held there unless it is for one of the outstanding citizens of the city when all the inhabitants of the city assemble there for this purpose. If a man finds it necessary to enter there for his own needs, to call someone, for instance, he should read or study something and then call him so that it should not appear as if he entered for his own needs. If he is incapable of reading or studying he should ask one of the children to read out to him something he is studying or he should simply stay there for a while before leaving since merely to sit there is a religious duty, as it is said: "Happy are they who dwell in Thy house" (Psalms 84:5). [To stay there in this connection means for the time it takes to enter through two doors.]

The exemption of scholars and their pupils with regard to eating is made in order to save them the time they would have to spend in going elsewhere for their meals. "Release of captives" refers to conditions in earlier times when Jews would occasionally be held for ransom by some petty tyrant. In such circumstances the Rabbis ruled that there is no greater religious duty than to raise the money for their ransom. The reference to "two doors" is based on a Talmudic passage and means the time it takes to enter through the two portals of the Synagogue, one in front of the other.

Some say that all we are told regarding the sanctity of Houses of Study applies only to public ones, like a Synagogue which is publicly owned, but there is not so much sanctity in a study room in a private house.

A man may have a study in his house in which he studies the Torah but since this a private arrangement it does not have the sanctity of a public building for prayer or study.

It is forbidden even to have a short nap in a Synagogue but in a House of Study this is permitted.

The reason for the distinction between a House of Study and a Synagogue in this connection is that in the former scholars spend a good deal of their day and it would be unreasonable to prevent them from having a short nap if they are tired.

It is permitted to eat or sleep in the Synagogue if it is for religious purposes. For this reason one may sleep in the Synagogue on Yom Kippur. It is also permitted to eat there if the purpose is for some other religious duty, for example, when they gather there for the purpose of making the year a leap-year.

In many Synagogues in former times (and occasionally even today) some people stayed the whole night in the Synagogue on Yom Kippur. The reference to the "leap-year" is to the ancient practice (before the calendar had been fixed as it is today) of having the leaders of the people gather in the Synagogue—if for some reason they wished to—exercising there their power to make the year a month longer. It was advised that a small feast be prepared to mark the occasion.

If a Synagogue has two doors one should not enter at one door and make a short cut by going out at the other, but if the public path went that way before the Synagogue was built it is permitted. It is also permitted to use the other door as a short cut if one did not enter with that intention. If one enters the Synagogue for prayer by one door it is permitted to go out by the other door.

Where the short-cut was already in existence there is no disrespect for the Synagogue if it continues to be used.

It is permitted to enter a Synagogue with a stick or a pouch or a money bag. Some say it is forbidden to enter a Synagogue with a long knife or with uncovered head.

A "long knife" means a knife used for the table i.e. there would be no objection to entering a Synagogue with a penknife. The reason given for the ruling is that the longer knife bears a resemblance to a sword or dagger and the Synagogue is a place dedicated to the promulgation of peace.

One may spit there provided the saliva is erased with one's foot or there is an absorbent material there so that the saliva is not seen.

This paragraph will strike many people today as strange. It must not be forgotten that many Synagogues in those days had floors of dirt or sand. We have been influenced by Western standards of decorum and Jews should not treat the Synagogue in a more disrespectful way than Christians treat the Church. It is for this reason that a number of present-day Rabbis rule that while there is no explicit prohibition against smoking in a Synagogue, it should nonetheless be strictly avoided.

It is proper to remove any clay that may be on one's shoes before entering the Synagogue and there should be no stains on one's person or clothes.

Some pious Jews in obedience to the law here went so far as to wear special clothes for the Synagogue.

Synagogue buildings should be treated with reverence by keeping them well swept and washed and it is customary to kindle lights there as a sign of reverence.

Care should be taken in the upkeep of the Synagogue in a manner befitting its dignity.

Even Synagogues in ruins must be treated with the same reverence as before because they still retain their sanctity except that in ruins they need not be swept and washed. If weeds grow on the ruins they should not be plucked out but left there in order to cause anguish to the public who will then be moved to rebuild.

The remark about weeds refers to the case of a single Synagogue in a community. If a new Synagogue is built to replace the old one it is permitted to sell the first.

If, when the Synagogue was built, it was expressly stated that it will be used also for profane purposes, it may be used for these purposes once it has fallen into ruin, but not while it is still in use for prayer. And even when in ruins it should not be used for any degrading purposes, to sow something there, for instance. Even an express statement from the beginning to this effect does not permit the use of a ruined Synagogue for the purpose of public business transactions.

All this applies only to Synagogues outside the Holy Land but no express condition can permit the use of Synagogues in the Holy Land for secular purposes.

In the land of Israel there is, in addition to the sanctity of the Synagogue, the sanctity of the land itself, the holy land. Because of this a greater degree of sanctity attaches itself to the Synagogues in the land of Israel.

One should take care not to use a room above a Synagogue for any permanent degrading purpose, to sleep there, for example. It is doubtful whether such a room may be used for other secular purposes. [All this only applies to a Synagogue built expressly for that purpose, but if a room in a house was set aside for use as a Synagogue after it had been built, it is permitted to sleep in the room above it.]

It would appear from this that it is not correct to build a Synagogue with apartments above it.

The obligation of studying Torah

The obligation to study Torah and the fees
that may be paid for such study.

This very long passage is for the most part self-explanatory. We add only such comments as are required in order to clear up any difficulties. It must be appreciated that, in the main, we have here a reflection of conditions very different from our own. Some of the statements are not quite to our taste and belong to a vanished world. But through the whole passage there breathes the great love of Torah study that was so marked a feature of the religion of the Rabbis.

Rabbi Moses Isserles' notes on Karo's text appear in brackets.

Every Jewish man is obliged to study the Torah, whether he is poor or rich, whether healthy or sick, whether young or very old. Even a poor man who begs at doors and even if he has a wife and family to support is obliged to set aside some time for Torah study during the day and at night, as it is said: "Thou shalt meditate therein day and night" (Joshua 1:8). (In an emergency the demands of this verse are satisfied if one recites the *Shema* in the morning and at night.) One who is unable to study either because he does not have the know-how or because he is very busy should support students of the Torah. [If he does this it is considered as if he had studied himself. A man may arrange with his friend that the friend will study the Torah while

he provides him with life's needs and he can then arrange to have a half share in the reward of his learning. But if one has already studied he cannot sell to another his portion for the sake of money he gives to him.]

Note how concerned the Rabbis were that even people unable to study should have a share in study of the Torah. At the least they could obtain this share by being of help in the support of students of the Torah.

A man should first study the Torah and then get married for if he marries first it will be impossible for him to study the Torah since he will have a millstone around his neck. But if it is impossible for him to be unmarried because he has a strong desire to marry he should marry first.

For how long should a man study? For the whole of his life. As it is said: "So that they do not fade from your mind as long as you live" (Deuteronomy 4:9). So long as a man does not study he forgets.

A man is obliged to divide his studies into three parts. One third should be for the study of the Written Torah, namely, the twenty four books of the Bible. Another third should be for the study of the Mishnah, which is the Oral Torah, and the Rabbinic comments on the Bible are included in this. Another third should be devoted to the study of the Talmud. This latter means that he should learn how to reason from one matter to another; how to infer one matter from another; how to compare one matter with another. He should investigate by means of the principles by which the Torah is explained until he knows the main ideas behind the precepts and how the different rules regarding that which is forbidden and that which is permitted are derived, and such other matters which we know by tradition. How can he do this? If he is a craftsman, working for three hours of the day and devoting nine hours to Torah study, he should spend three hours on the Written Torah, three on the Oral Torah and three on the science of inference. All this applies only to man's studies at the beginning. But once a man has grown in Torah knowledge so that he no longer needs to study the Written Torah or to engage himself frequently in the study of the Oral Torah he should read only occasionally at fixed times in the Written Torah and the Oral in order not to forget anything of the Torah laws and should devote all his time to the Talmud alone according to the capacity of his intellect and the serenity of his mind. [Some say that a man fulfills his duty with regard to the whole of this if he studies the Babylonian Talmud which contains Bible, Mishnah and Gemara. A man should only study Bible, Mishnah, Gemara and the Codes and through these he will acquire both this world and the next, but he should not study other sciences. However, it is permitted to study other sciences occasionally provided that this does not involve the reading of heretical books. The Sages call this "walking in Paradise." A man should not walk in Paradise until he has filled his stomach with meat and wine, that is, to know that which is forbidden and that which is permitted and the laws of the precepts.]

The example is given of a workman who devotes three hours a day to his work and nine to the Torah. This is no doubt an exaggeration but that it should be given speaks volumes for the Rabbinic attachment to learning. The question of secular learning discussed here has had a long history. Nowadays, of course, most Jews think it right to be well educated in general subjects. Rabbi Isserles calls secular learning "walking in Paradise." But others understand by this term the study of the Kabbalah, the Jewish mystical teachings, which only one who has mastered the classic tradition should seek to study.

In a place where it is the custom to teach the Bible for a fee it is permitted to teach for a fee but it is forbidden to teach the Oral Torah for a fee. If a man cannot find anyone to teach him free of charge he may pay a fee to be taught. But even though he himself was obliged to pay for his studies he should not say later: "Just as I had to pay for my studies I shall teach for a fee" but he should teach others free of charge. As for the practice nowadays to teach everything for a fee—it is permitted if he has no other means of support and even if he has it is permitted if the fee is for the time he spends, that is, where it is clear that he has left aside all other business to devote himself to teaching. [It is permitted to accept fees for teaching any of the innovations of the Scribes.]

The reference to "innovations of the Scribes" is to new laws introduced by the Rabbis of succeeding generations. For example, the Rabbis in the eleventh century promulgated a new law forbidding polygamy. Or in an earlier generation the Rabbis ruled that a wife must receive a sum of money for her support if she is divorced.

A woman who studies the Torah has reward for this but it is not as great as the reward of a man who studies, since she is under no legal obligation to study. Even though she has reward for her studies, the Rabbis advised against a man teaching the Torah to his daughter, because the majority of women cannot concentrate properly on their studies and they interpret the Torah in a stupid way in accordance with the poverty of their minds. The Sages say: "Whoever teaches the Torah to his daughter it is as if he taught her folly" (this means sinfulness). This only applies to the Oral Torah but with regard to the Written Torah he should not teach it to her in the first instance but if he does it is not considered as if he had taught her folly. [However a woman is obliged to study the laws appertaining to women. A woman is under no legal obligation to have her children taught the Torah. Nevertheless, if she helps her son or her husband to study the Torah she divides the reward with them.]

The references to the woman have to be understood against the background of the time when women did not normally take part in social or communal activities to anything like the extent they do as a matter of course nowadays. Note the interesting point at the beginning that one who carries out a duty he must do is superior to one who performs a good deed voluntarily. Can you give a reason for this?

One must not teach the Torah to an unworthy pupil but one must first restore him to the right path and lead him in upright ways and test him. One may then bring him to the House of Study and teach him.

One should not study at the feet of a Rabbi who does not walk in the right way, even if he is a great sage whose wisdom is needed by all the people, until he returns to the good way.

How is the Torah taught? The Rabbi sits at the top surrounded like a crown by his pupils in order that they all can see the Rabbi and hear what he has to say. The Rabbi should not sit on a chair with his pupils on the ground but they should all either sit on chairs or all on the ground. [Some say that this only applies when the pupils have been ordained. The laws regarding a Rabbi who teaches through an interpreter are referred to in the sources but Rabbi Karo does not mention them since they are infrequent.]

The reference to an "interpreter" is to the practice in Talmudic times for the sage to say only a few words which would be expounded at much greater length by an official of the college. Rabbi Isserles suggests that Rabbi Karo has omitted these laws from the Shulḥan Arukh because scholars in his day no longer followed this method of study.

The Rabbi should not be angry with his pupils if they do not understand but he should repeat the matter over and over again until they grasp the proper depth of the law. The pupil should not say that he understands when he does not but should ask over and over again. And if the Rabbi is angry with him he should say: "Rabbi it is the Torah and I want to know it but my mind is inadequate."

A pupil should not be ashamed if his friend grasps the matter the first or second time whereas he does not grasp it even after many times, for once a pupil is ashamed in this matter he will go in and out of the House of Study without ever learning anything. It is with regard to this that the Sages say: "One who is ashamed will never learn and one who is quick-tempered cannot teach." This only applies where the pupils do not grasp the subject because it is so hard or because their minds are not sufficiently keen. But if the Rabbi notices that the pupils are lazy and insufficiently concerned with the Torah and this is why they cannot grasp the subject, he is obliged to be angry with them and to put them to shame in order to make them more keen. It is in this connection that it was said: "Cast gall into the pupils." Therefore, it is improper for the Rabbi to be frivolous in the presence of his pupils or to make jokes with them or eat and drink with them. Let him act so that they might have respect for him and learn quickly from him.

Questions should not be put to the Rabbi until he has time to settle down after he has entered the House of Study and the pupil should not ask any questions until he has settled down. Two pupils should not ask their questions together. They should only put questions to the Rabbi on the subject they are studying not on some other topic in order not to embarrass him. A Rabbi should try to trick his pupils by the questions he asks them or by the things he does in order to see if they remember what he has taught them. It goes without saying that he may set them questions on topics other than those they are studying in order to make them keen.

Questions should not be put while standing nor should replies be given while standing. [But some say that when a question is put on a matter of law it should be put while standing.] Questions and answers should not be given from above or from a distance or from behind the older scholars. All questions should be to the point and with respect, but no more than three questions on any one topic should be put at one time.

If two pupils ask a question, one of them relevant and the other not relevant, the reply should be addressed to the relevant question. If a practical question is asked and a theoretical the reply should be addressed to the practical. If one is a question of law and the other of exposition the reply should be addressed to the question of law. If one question is on exposition and the other on *Aggadah* the reply should be addressed to the question on exposition. *Aggadah* and an argument from the minor to the major, the reply should be addressed to the latter. An argument from the minor to the major and a comparison, the reply should be addressed to the former.

The references are to different matters of study. Aggadah is the non-legal material of the Talmud i.e. its stories, philosophy, ethics, history and so on. An "argument from the minor to the major" is where an attempt is made to prove that A is so because B is so. The formula is: If B which is less severe is so, then A which is more severe is certainly so. To give a modern example: If a shop assistant earns ten dollars the manager is certainly entitled to at least ten dollars. A "comparison" is where a word in one passage

of Scripture is made to throw light on a similar word in another
passage

If one of the two questioners was a sage and the other a pupil the reply should be addressed to the sage. If one was a pupil and the other an ignoramus the reply should be addressed to the pupil. If both were sages or both pupils or both ignoramuses or if two people asked on different topics or there were two questions to be answered or two decisions to make, the Rabbi has the right to reply to whichever he chooses. [An illegitimate child who is a scholar takes precedence over a person of priestly family who is an ignoramus.]

One should not sleep in the House of Study and whoever nods in the House of Study his learning is torn into pieces. As it is said: "And drowsiness shall clothe a man with rags" (Proverbs 23:21).

One should speak only of Torah in the House of Study. Even if someone sneezes in the House of Study one should not say: "Bless you." A House of Study is more sacred than a Synagogue.

Note the typical Rabbinic teaching that a House of Study
(Bet Ha-Midrash) has a greater degree of sanctity than a Synagogue.
For instance the Rabbis say that it is forbidden to run from a
House of Study to a Synagogue but not vice versa.

The study of the Torah is equal to all the other precepts. If a man is faced with a good deed and the study of the Torah then he should not be interrupted in his studies if the good deed can be carried out by someone else. Otherwise he should carry out the good deed and return to his studies.

On judgment day a man is first judged on whether he studied the Torah and only afterwards on his other deeds.

A man should always study the Torah even if his motives are not worthy, for from study out of unworthy motives he will come to study out of worthy ones.

*These remarks are the summary of a long debate which still
continues. The ideal aim is to study for its own sake but supposing
a man studies because of the material gains this will bring him—
people will respect him, he may become rich, and the like.
Some argued that it is better not to study at all than to use the
Torah for selfish ends. But the view which won out is the one
recorded here that motives should at first be ignored. The important
thing is to become a learned Jew and then one will come to love
the Torah for its own sake.*

The words of Torah do not endure among those who are lazy in
their pursuit and not among those who study in the midst of pleasure
or when eating and drinking but only in the man who kills himself
over the Torah, always giving pain to himself and denying sleep to
his eyes and slumber to his eyelids. [A man should not have the
intention of studying the Torah and gaining fame and riches at the
same time for whoever allows this notion to enter his head will never
attain the crown of the Torah. But he should make the study of Torah
permanent and his work casual and should do little business in order
to have time for study. He should remove from his heart the pleasure
which time brings and do only sufficient work each day to enable
him to exist if he has nothing to eat and for the rest of the day and
night he should study the Torah. It is very praiseworthy that a man
live off the labor of his hands, as it is said: "When thou shalt eat the
labor of thine hands" (Psalms 128:2). Whoever thinks of studying the
Torah without doing any work and to live off charity profanes God's
name and degrades the Torah for it is forbidden to have any material
benefit from the Torah. Any Torah that is not accompanied by work
causes sin and such a man will eventually become a robber. All this
applies only to a healthy person who is able to work or do a little
business in order to support himself but an old or sick person is
permitted to have material benefit from his Torah and people may
support him. Others say it is permitted even in the case of a healthy
man. It is therefore the custom in all the places in which Israel dwells
that the Rabbi of a town has a salary and is supported by the
inhabitants of the city in order to avoid the need for him to do work
in front of people which degrades the Torah in the eyes of the
populace. But this only applies to a sage who needs it but not to a

rich man. Some are more lenient still and they allow a sage and his pupils to accept a stipend from generous givers in order that the scholars be helped to study the Torah comfortably. However, anyone who can easily support himself by the work of his hands and study the Torah follows the saintly life if he does so. But this is not possible for everyone for it is impossible for most men to study the Torah and become wise in learning while supporting himself by his work at the same time. All this is only permitted if it is in the nature of a communal stipend or fixed amount but a scholar should not accept gifts from others. When the Rabbis say that whoever brings gifts to a sage it is as if he had brought the first ripe fruits to the Temple, they refer to small presents, since it is the custom to bring small presents to a man of importance even if he is an ignoramus. A scholar may also taste of that which he has permitted in order to demonstrate the correctness of his ruling. But it is forbidden for him to accept a large gift from something he has permitted. "One who uses the crown will depart from the world." But some say that this means one who uses sacred names for magical purposes. It is permitted for a scholar to make known who he is in a place where he is unknown.]

The opening words are a particularly vivid way of saying that great sacrifices are demanded of the scholar prepared to spend many years in study. Note the lengthy comment by Rabbi Isserles. The truth is that scholars like the great Maimonides in the Middle Ages earned their living in other ways and refused to benefit materially from their learning. But eventually experience proved that this was was only for the few. From the fourteenth century onwards it became the established practice for Jewish communities to support their scholars.

There is an unfailing promise that whoever studies in the House of Study will not easily forget what he has learned. Whoever labors over his learning in private will become wise, as it is said: "Wisdom is with the modest" (Proverbs 11:2). Whoever raises his voice while studying will find that his learning endures but one who reads silently will soon forget.

Note the advice to study in a loud voice. This has been virtually forgotten in our day but there is still much psychological sense in what is said here.

Whoever wishes to attain the crown of the Torah should be thrifty with all his nights not wasting any of them in sleep or eating and drinking or conversation and so forth but in words of wisdom and the study of the Torah. [For a man only gains most of his wisdom by night. A man should begin to study by night from the fifteenth day of Av onwards and he who does not add to his nights from this one will depart from the world.]

The reference to "departing from the world" is, of course, hyperbolic. The fifteenth of Av, which generally comes about midsummer, is about when the longer nights begin. During the summer there is not much time for night studies.

Fire will consume any house in which Torah is not heard at night.

This paragraph is similarly hyperbolic.

Whoever is able to study the Torah and does not do so or anyone who has studied the Torah and then goes out into the world and its vanities and leaves the Torah behind him despises God's word. [It is forbidden to engage in pointless conversation.]

The Rabbis were so concerned that the Torah be studied that they tended to frown on any pointless conversation as a waste of time which could profitably be spent studying the Torah.

Whoever sets the Torah aside when he is rich will eventually set it aside when he is poor but whoever keeps the Torah when he is poor will eventually keep it when he is rich. [Whenever a man completes a tractate of the Talmud it is a religious duty to rejoice and make a party and such a party is called a "religious feast." It is forbidden to study the Torah in dirty places. It is therefore forbidden for a scholar to stand in dirty places in order that he should not think there on words of Torah. However, he is allowed to enter a bathhouse even while he is reflecting on a complicated matter of law and we are not afraid that he will continue to reflect on it in the bathhouse. For a scholar is careful not to think on words of Torah in such a place.]

Respect for scholars and the aged

*The different ways of showing respect to scholars
and elderly people.*

Rabbi Moses Isserles' notes on Karo's text appear in brackets.

**It is a positive precept to rise before any sage even if he is not an old
man but a youthful scholar and even if he is not one's teacher
[provided that he is a greater scholar from whom one can learn]. It
is also a religious duty to rise before an old man, that is to say
someone who is seventy years of age [even if he is an ignorant man
provided he is not wicked].**

*In Leviticus chapter 19 verse 32 we read: "Thou shalt rise before
the aged and show deference to the old." By the term "the old"
(zaken) the Rabbis understand not necessarily an old man but one
learned in the Torah (as in the Biblical expression: "the elders of
Israel" i.e. the leaders and teachers). Consequently the duty of
rising as a mark of respect applies to both an old man and to a
young man learned in the Torah. The one is rich in learning; the
other rich in experience of life. This paragraph defines the two terms.
The scholar is even a young man and the "old man" is one who is
at least seventy years of age. Rising before the old man has nothing
to do with his learning or lack of it. Even if he is ignorant one must
rise before him, but not if he is a wicked man for it is unfitting
to show marks of respect to such a person.*

When does the duty of rising apply? From the time he comes within one's four cubits until he moves out of his vicinity. If he is riding it is as if he were walking.

A cubit is about two feet in length. The remark about riding means that one should not only apply the law to a sage or old man walking in the street but even to one who was riding.

It is forbidden to close one's eyes before he enters one's four cubits so as to avoid the necessity of rising when he comes into one's four cubits.

A man might say that the law only obliges me to rise if I see the sage or the old man. Very well, then, I shall shut my eyes tightly whenever I sense that one of these is about to appear. The Shulḥan Arukh states that this is an unworthy attempt at defeating the spirit of the law while obeying its letter.

One does not rise before them in a public convenience or in a bathhouse. It is written: "Thou shalt rise and show deference" (Leviticus 19:32), which means that rising is only to be carried out when it is deferential. [This only applies to the inner rooms of the bathhouse but one does rise in the outer rooms.]

There is nothing respectful in trying to show signs of respect in places like a public convenience or a public bathhouse. However, this applies only to the inner rooms where people are undressed. But in the outer rooms where they congregate socially with their clothes on the law does apply. A modern analogy would be, at the bar of a social club but not at the swimming pool.

Workmen while engaged in their work are not obliged to rise before sages. If they were working for others they are not permitted to be strict on themselves and to rise nevertheless.

Workmen are exempt from the law even if they are working for themselves. In the latter case they may, if they wish, be strict on themselves and refuse to avail themselves of the dispensation and rise. However, if they have been hired to do work for someone else they have no right to be strict, because by so doing they are wasting not their own time but that of their employer.

It is improper for a sage to bother the community by passing in front of its members intentionally so that they will be obliged to rise before him, but he should pass quickly before them in order that they be not obliged to rise before him for a long period. But if he goes on a roundabout way so as not to pass before them at all it is meritorious.

Although people who rise before a sage or an old man are carrying out a religious duty he should not take advantage of this by causing them frequent bother. He should try to pass by as quickly as possible and if he can avoid passing by at all he should by all means do so.

Even a youthful sage must rise before a man of ripe old age but he is not obliged to rise to his full height, only sufficient to mark his respect. Marks of respect through words uttered should be paid even to a heathen who is aged and he should be given a hand to support him.

A sage is not, of course, exempted from the duty of rising before an old man but out of respect for his learning he is exempted from rising to his full height. Even heathens (in Rabbinic times this meant not only people who were not Jews but idolators) should be treated with respect if they are old. As a Rabbi in the Talmud put it: "How much experience have these men gone through."

Two sages or two old men are not obliged to rise before one another but some token of respect should be paid. [Even a teacher should pay some token of respect to his pupil.]

This paragraph explains itself. The point is that respect is being paid not so much to the individual sage or old man but to old age and to learning.

When one notices a sage passing by one is not obliged to rise before him until he reaches one's four cubits and one can sit down again once the sage has moved out of the vicinity. But if the sage is his permanent teacher he should rise as soon as he sees him and should not sit down again until he is either out of sight or has sat down in his place.

*A permanent teacher is defined as one from whom a person has
learned most of what he knows.*

**A sage outstanding for his learning is to be treated as a permanent
teacher. [One who is great in his generation and renowned in his
generation for learning is considered outstanding in learning.]**
*A really outstanding sage is treated as the teacher of his entire
generation.*

**It is necessary to rise before a sage even if one is studying the Torah
at the time.**
*One might have argued that since the purpose of rising is to show
respect for the Torah there is no need to rise if one is already
showing that respect in the best way possible by actually studying
the Torah.*

**Even a sage outstanding for his learning is permitted to rise before
one who is noted for his good deeds.**
*Normally a sage is not permitted to rise before an unscholarly man
who is not aged because he must respect his own dignity as a
bearer of the Torah. But he may rise in order to pay his respects
to a man noted for his good deeds for good deeds are after all
the purpose of Torah study or, at least, a very important part of it.*

**If one noticed a head of the court passing by, one should rise as
soon as he comes into sight and remain standing until he passes out
of one's four cubits.**
*The terms in the following paragraphs are taken from the Talmud.
They refer to specific offices in Palestine and these were no longer
in vogue at the time of the Shulḥan Arukh, but the original rules
as found in the Talmud are nevertheless recorded. The "head of the
court" was second only to the Prince in the leadership of the
whole people (or, in any event, those who followed the Rabbis).
The Prince was a direct descendant of the great Hillel. The "sage"
is the special lecturer at the college.*

**If one saw the Prince one should rise as soon as he comes into sight
and should not sit down again until he either sits in his place or**

moves out of sight. In all these cases if they waive their rights there is no longer any obligation to rise. Nevertheless it still is good to respect them and to rise a little when they pass by.

In all cases where respect is to be paid it need not be if the recipient decides that he does not wish it.

When the Prince enters the college they should all rise and should not sit down again until he instructs them to do so. When the head of the court enters they should form rows on either side of him until he occupies his seat.

Notice how the Rabbis laid down rules not only for respect for learning but for degrees of learning.

The sons of sages and their pupils, if they are needed by the community, may step over the heads of the people in order to reach their place. But it is not praiseworthy for a pupil of the sages to enter last or to go out to attend to his own needs and then return to his place.

When people occupy high office their sons and pupils generally find that they, too, share in the glory. But they must not abuse this. They may only "step over the heads" of the people if they are required for the services they alone can perform for the community. "Stepping over the heads" evidently means walking into the college while the "people" are sitting down.

The sons of sages whose fathers have been appointed community leaders may enter and sit in front of their fathers with their faces turned toward their fathers if they have an opinion to express. But if they have no opinion to express they should turn their faces toward the people.

When the young people sit near the top with their faces toward their fathers this will mean that their back will be toward the people. This is disrespectful and is only permitted if they have something to contribute to the deliberations of their elders.

If a sage outstanding for his learning but young in years is together with a man of outstanding age who has a little learning, then in a sitting for the purposes of justice or study of the Torah wisdom takes precedence, so that the youthful sage sits at the top and is asked to speak first. But at a banquet or a wedding feast age is given precedence and the older man sits at the top. But if the sage is outstanding in learning and the old man is not outstandingly old then wisdom always takes precedence. If the old man is outstandingly old and the sage is not outstanding in learning then age always take precedence since the old man has a little learning. If neither of them is outstanding, the one in learning the other in age, the old man always takes precedence.

This paragraph deals with cases where there is a question of precedence. The different cases are easily understood. A "sitting for the purpose of justice" means at a court of law.

Reclining and drinking at the Passover Seder

The laws of eating and drinking at the home service on Passover.

Rabbi Moses Isserles' notes on Karo's text appear in brackets.

A man's table should be prepared while it is still day time so that he can eat as soon as it gets dark. Even if he is studying in the House of Study he should rise and go home because it is a religious duty to eat as soon as one can and before the children fall asleep. However, Kiddush should not be recited until it is dark.

The point here is that an essential feature of the Seder *service on Passover is for the children to ask questions and have them answered. But, says Rabbi Karo, the Kiddush, the beginning of the* Seder, *should not be started until nightfall.*

He should do all he can to adorn the table with beautiful tableware and he should prepare the place where he is to sit so that he will be able to sit in a reclining posture in the manner of free men. [Even a poor man who has no cushions should sit on a long bench so that he can recline.]

Since Passover is the festival of freedom the Rabbis ruled that each Jew should recline while eating his meal as free men did in Greek and Roman times.

When reclining he should not lean backwards or forwards nor should he recline on his right side but on his left. [There is no difference in this matter between a left-handed person and any other person.]

Reclining was always on the left hand because this was the easiest position for eating.

A woman need not recline unless she were of outstanding importance. [All our womenfolk are considered of outstanding importance. However, they still do not recline for they rely on the view of Rebiah who writes that nowadays there is no need to recline.]

Rabbi Karo, following chiefly oriental views, makes a distinction between a woman of importance, who would recline at meals, and a woman of less importance. Rabbi Isserles, following German scholars, is more chivalrous. All our women, says he, are important. However, the custom is for women not to recline because they follow the view of Rebiah who argues that reclining has no meaning in countries where it is never the custom to recline at meals. The point here is that according to Rebiah there is no special rule of reclining at the Seder. The only rule is that men have to sit as free men at the Seder and since free men recline it is necessary to recline. But in a society where free men do not recline at meals, reclining need not be resorted to since it is no sign of freedom. It is rather as if in our society the Rabbis ruled that a man should demonstrate his freedom by smoking a fat cigar. If that were the rule it would obviously not apply to a society where there is no cigar smoking.

Rebiah is the acronym of Rabbi Eliezer Ben Joel Ha-Levi the famous German Talmudist who lived from the second half of the twelfth century to the first half of the thirteenth.

A son is required to recline in the presence of his father even if the father is his main teacher. But a pupil must not recline in the presence of his teacher, even if he is not his main teacher, unless given permission to do so. A scholar outstanding in his generation is to be treated as if he were his teacher, even if he had learned nothing from him, and he need not recline. [However, this only applies where they both eat at the same table, but where they eat at separate tables he must recline.]

It was considered disrespectful to recline in the presence of an older or wiser man, hence these rules.

One's retainer must also recline.

It might have been argued that since one's servant is waiting on the table he need not recline but he, too, is a Jew and has to keep the various rules of the Seder.

Whoever is required to recline has not carried out his duty if he did not recline and is obliged to eat and drink all over again while reclining. [Some say that nowadays when it is not normal to recline at meals, the Rebiah is great enough to be relied upon in changing the practice. Therefore if one has already eaten and drunk without reclining he is considered as having carried out his duty. It seems to me that if he did not recline while drinking the third or fourth cup he should not drink again while reclining for this would look as if he added to the number of cups. But in the case of the first two cups he should drink again without reciting the benediction. The same applies to eating matzah. **He should try to recline while eating the whole meal.]**

Rabbi Karo is so strict that he demands the whole thing to be done again if reclining were omitted. This is because he generally follows the Spanish authorities. But Rabbi Isserles, who generally follows the German authorities, argues that since such a great authority as Rebiah rules in any case that it is no longer necessary to recline in our lands, he can waive the requirement of doing it again if reclining had been omitted. It looks as if one is adding to the number of cups if one drinks extra cups after the third or fourth which are partaken of after the meal. It would not appear this way with the others which are partaken of either before or during the meal.

He must drink the four cups in order but if he drank them one after another outside the order he has not carried out his duty.

Seder means "order" and there is a recognized place in the services at which each of the cups are to be partaken of. Obviously it will not do to drink all four at once.

The amount of wine in each cup should be a quarter of a *log* after it has been diluted [if he wishes to dilute it]. He should either drink the whole of the cup or most of it. If the cup contains many quarters, as many people may drink from it as the number of quarters it contains. But some say that it is always necessary to drink most of the cup even if it contains many quarters. [It is necessary to drink the amount required without pausing too long between sips.]

A log is a liquid measure obtained by estimating the displacement of six eggs. Hence a "quarter" is the amount of wine displaced by an egg and a half. It was frequently the custom in those days to dilute the wine with water before drinking it.

Even one who does not drink wine because it does not agree with him or because he hates it must force himself to drink in order to fulfill the religious duty of drinking four cups.

Since wine is the main symbol of freedom on this night everyone should do his utmost to drink the four cups. Obviously this rule does not apply to one who becomes ill from drinking wine.

It is good to obtain red wine [unless a superior white wine is available].

If red and white wine are of the same quality red should be preferred because Scripture speaks of wine as red. If, however, the white wine obtainable is of superior vintage it should be preferred, says Rabbi Isserles.

The duty of drinking four cups of wine can be fulfilled with spiced wine or boiled wine.

It might have been argued that this is not what one drinks when one generally partakes of wine.

Even a man so poor that he lives by begging must either sell his garment or borrow money or hire himself to do a job in order to obtain wine for the four cups.

Further evidence of how much significance the Rabbis attached to drinking wine on this night. In fact in most Jewish communities

the poor people are provided by the community with wine
and matzot and the other Passover foods.

**Women are also obliged to drink the four cups and to carry out
all the duties of this night.**

The general rule is that women need not carry out religious duties
which have to be carried out at a particular time. (The reason
may be because they are too busy with the home and children
to be tied down in this way.) But the Seder eve is an exception.

**Children old enough to be taught should be given each his own
cup of wine. [One should not take a cup with a narrow mouth
because it is impossible to drink a quarter at once. In any event
such a cup should not be used for Grace after Meals.]**

It is an important principle of Judaism that children should gradually
be trained to keep Jewish observances.

**It is a religious duty to hand round to the children parched ears of
corn and nuts in order that they should see something unusual
going on and ask questions.**

Since so much centers around the questions of the children on this
night every encouragement should be given them to become curious
about what is going on.

Harmful words

The laws of things which should not be said.

Rabbi Solomon Ganzfried, 1804—1886, is the author of the Abridged Shulḥan Arukh, which, as its name implies, is a much shorter version of Rabbi Joseph Karo's large work. Rabbi Ganzfried drew not only on the Shulḥan Arukh but on many other sources of Jewish law. The little book became very popular and has been reprinted many times.

Just as it is forbidden to wrong another in buying and selling it is forbidden to wrong him with words. As it is said: "Do not wrong one another, but fear thy God" (Leviticus 25:17). The reference here is to wronging with words. It is a worse offense to wrong with words than to wrong in buying and selling for in the one case restitution is possible, in the other it is impossible; in the one case the victim is only cheated of his money, in the other he is wronged in his person. Whoever cries out against one who wrongs him with words is answered immediately. It is especially necessary not to wrong one's wife with words since women are sensitive by nature and are easily moved to tears. God is annoyed when anyone is made to weep and the gates of tears are never closed.

According to the Rabbis of the Talmud the verse in Leviticus 25:17 does not refer to cheating in business since other verses deal with this specifically. Hence they speak of "wronging with words" i.e. saying harsh, wounding things so as to cause someone pain and anguish. Two reasons are given for treating "wronging with words" as a worse offense than robbing someone of his money by cheating. When a man has been cheated out of his money the wrong is not necessarily irrevocable. It is possible to take the thief to court and the victim can recover his loss. But words which wound cannot be recalled. They continue to hurt the victim. The second reason is that cheating a man of his money does not affect the person himself, whereas harmful words affect the person himself profoundly. Do you recall Shakespeare's lines?

> "Who steals my purse steals trash; 'tis something, nothing;
> 'Twas mine, 'tis his, and has been slave to thousands;
> But he that filches from me my good name
> Robs me of that which not enriches him,
> And makes me poor indeed."

The meaning of the sentence about "crying out" is that God is, as it were, always on the side of the victim wronged by words and when he cries out to God in pain God will answer him. The "gates of tears" are the gates of Heaven which are sometimes closed (sometimes prayers are not answered) but which always open to tears.

What is meant by "wronging with words"? A man should not ask his neighbor how much he wants for a certain object if he has no intention of buying it. If someone was looking around for corn to buy he should not tell him: "Go to so-and-so" knowing full well that that person has no corn to sell. If, God forbid, his neighbor was suffering, he should not say to him, as Job's friends said to him "Remember, I pray thee, who ever perished, being innocent?" (Job 4:7). (Job's friends only said this because they saw that Job questioned God's justice.) If someone asked him a question which involves learning he should not turn to an unlearned person to ask him what he thinks about it. There are other examples all of which cause someone's heart to ache.

Some illustrations are now given of "wronging with words." To bother a shopkeeper with questions about how much his goods cost when one had no intention of buying is to build up his hopes of making a sale without intending to satisfy them and is to "wrong with words." Similarly, to mislead a prospective customer by directing him to someone who cannot supply the goods he seeks is to "wrong with words." If a man has repented of the wrong he has done it should all be forgotten. Some of the Rabbis say that a sinner who repents is greater than a man who has never sinned. In any event it is quite wrong to remind such a man of his former bad ways. He is bound to be very sensitive about these and it is wounding in the extreme to show that others are aware of his earlier misdeeds and are determined not to allow him to forget them Nowadays this would surely apply to someone who has been in prison but has made a fresh, honest start in life. He should be given every encouragement and not reminded of his lapse or his "record." Job's friends (Job's comforters as they are called) when they saw that the good man, Job, was in pain and suffered much, tried to defend God's justice by suggesting that Job was punished because of his sins. This is a very cruel thing to do. The truth is that we do not know why God brings sufferings upon men but we believe that God is good and knows what is right. But it is clear that sometimes very good men suffer, so by suggesting whenever a man suffers that it is God's punishment for his sins is heartless and only provides the poor man with further reason for torment. Rabbi Ganzfried adds in brackets that Job's friends only did this because they felt that Job had gone too far in hinting that God was not just. Finally, Rabbi Ganzfried gives the example of pretending to call in the help of an unlearned man to solve an intellectual problem, so as to embarrass him.

If a person has an unpleasant nickname, even if he has become used to it and is no longer embarrassed when it is uttered, another person should not call him by this nickname if his intention is to embarrass him. To do so would be to offend against "wronging with words."
This paragraph explains itself. Obviously it is wrong to call a man by a nickname he hates. But intention matters so that even if he has learned to live with his nickname it is wrong to call him by it if the intention is malicious.

It is forbidden to steal people's hearts (this means to deceive with words even when no financial loss results) and this applies to non-

Jew as well as to Jew. For this reason it is forbidden to sell meat which has not been ritually slaughtered in the proper way if the buyer imagines that he is purchasing meat which has been correctly slaughtered. If a man sells another an object with a blemish it is necessary that the buyer be informed of the blemish even if the object is worth the price asked even with the blemish. (But deceit does not apply to a gift.)

The expression "stealing the heart" is biblical (see Genesis 31:20). It is an idiomatic expression for misleading people. According to Jewish teaching every human being is created in God's image so that Rabbi Ganzfried, following the Talmud, states that there is no difference whether the victim is Jew or non-Jew. Some people are only prepared to behave by the highest ethical standards where their own group is concerned, but Judaism demands that they be applied to all men. It is true that in times of persecution some Jewish teachers had harsh things to say about their persecutors but Judaism has never lost this basic idea. Meat from an animal slaughtered in the proper manner (Shehitah) looks no different from other meat but it is obviously a case of cheating to sell one as the other. A modern example of this would be a shop or restaurant which advertises as kosher but which sells terefah. A further example given by Rabbi Ganzfried is when a man sells an object with a flaw, which cannot easily be detected, without informing the customer. The point he makes is that this is forbidden as a deceitful act even if the price is such that there is no actual financial loss. In a bracket Rabbi Ganzfried says that this would not apply to the case of a man who gives his friend a gift with an undetected flaw since it is still a gift for all that.

A man should not invite his neighbor to eat at his table if he knows quite well that the invitation will be refused. He should not pretend to give him a present knowing full well that he will not accept it. And the same applies to whenever he does similar things, saying one thing with his mouth and meaning something different in his heart, showing his neighbor that he intends to honor him but not really meaning it deep in his heart. A man's mouth and heart should be as one and he should train his lips to speak honestly, his spirit to be one of integrity and his heart pure.

Some further examples of deceit are now given. If a man wishes to pose as a good host but only invites someone to his table because he knows that he will refuse, this is to deceive. In our day, for instance, a man may wish to impress a non-smoker with his generosity by offering him a cigar, the offer only being made because it is known that it will be refused. The Rabbinic expression used is that a man's heart and mouth should be in accord. He should mean what he says. It should be noted that these are not examples of downright lies, which are easy to detect, but to the kind of dishonesty from which one point of view is far worse in that it is utterly misleading.

The Responsa

IN SPITE OF the many Codes of Jewish law produced throughout the ages, and in spite of the many decisions found in the Talmud, there were bound to be numerous cases, due to new conditions or unusual circumstances, in which no direct decision was available. In these cases less confident scholars would turn for guidance to recognized experts in the law. Questions were addressed to these experts and they replied. In the course of time a scholar who had given such answers or his pupils or sons would collect his replies and publish the collection. Thus today there are thousands of Responsa collections. Responsa means "answer." The Hebrew name for this type of Jewish literature is *She'elot u-Teshuvot*, "Questions and Answers."

The various codifiers would make use of the Responsa collections in compiling their Codes. Then new questions would arise and further Responsa would be produced. The process continues to the present day.

It should be noted that the scholars to whom the questions were addressed were not necessarily men holding official Rabbinic positions of importance. Sometimes men who had an inferior position or no position at all, but who were renowned for their expertise in Jewish law, were sent questions by their fellow-Rabbis and gradually became the authors of Responsa collections. So, though no one ever appointed or elected certain scholars to positions of authority in Jewish law, the fact that other scholars recognized some men as worthy of being consulted gave them their pre-eminence. That kept a certain democracy in Jewish law as well as a pattern of authority.

Since the Responsa literature covers the development of Jewish law over a 1200 year span, it provides us with valuable information about the religious, social, economic, moral and political life of Jewish communities at different periods of Jewish history.

CHAPTER 27

Are Muslims idolators?

The status of Muslims in Jewish law and the treatment of converts.

The following passage is taken from a Responsum of Moses Maimonides (1135–1204), edited by Joshua Blau, Jerusalem, 1960, No. 448, Vol. II, 11, pages 725–728. It is a question asked of Maimonides by Rabbi Obadiah, a convert to Judaism, and Maimonides' reply thereto.

QUESTION: **The question concerns the Arabs. You argued that they are not idolators but your teacher argues that they are idolators and that the stones they throw in their place of worship are to** *Mercury.* **Furthermore he answered you in an unworthy manner so that you became upset and embarrassed and he applied to you the verse: "Answer a fool according to his folly" (Proverbs 26:5).**

REPLY: **The Arabs are in no way idolators. Idolatry has long been cut off from their mouths and hearts and they accept the unity of God as it should be accepted, a unity without falsehood. Because they falsely accuse us of entertaining the notion that God has a son, shall we falsely retaliate by saying that they are idolators? The same Torah which testifies of them: "Whose mouth speaketh falsehood, And** their right hand is a hand of lying" (Psalms 144:8) testified of us: "The remnant of Israel shall not do iniquity, Nor speak lies, Neither shall a deceitful tongue be found in their mouth" (Zephaniah 3:13).

If someone were to argue that the house in which they worship is a house of idolatry and an idol is hidden therein which their ancestors used to worship, what of it! Those who worship there today have only God in mind. Our Rabbis have already explained in tractate *Sanhedrin* (61b) that if a man bows down before a house of idolatry thinking it is a Synagogue his heart is directed toward God. The same applies to these Arabs today. Idolatry has been cut off from the mouths of all of them including the women and children. Their folly is only with regard to other matters which I cannot state explicitly out of fear of wicked and iniquitous Jews. But with regard to the unity of God they have no mistake at all.

It is true that the Arabs in these places in former times did have three types of gods—*Peor, Mercury* and *Kemosh*. They themselves admit this and call these three gods by their Arabic names. *Peor* was worshipped by people exposing themselves before it or by bowing before it with the head low and the back elevated as the Arabs do nowadays when they pray. *Mercury* was worshipped by throwing stones. *Kemosh* was worshipped by uncovering the head and by refraining from wearing a garment with stitches. These matters are all explained and stated explicitly in our writings from former times that these belong to Arabic worship. But the present-day Arabs say that the reason they uncover their heads and refrain from wearing a garment with stitches is in order to humble their hearts before God and to remind themselves of how man will rise from his grave. And the reason they throw stones to the devil is in order to confuse him. Some of the more sophisticated of them give a different reason and say that at one time there were idols there and they throw stones at the places where the idols were as if to say, we do not believe in the idols that were there and as a token of how we despise them we throw stones at them. Others simply say that it is an old custom. To sum it up—even though all these things had their origins in idolatry, nowhere in the whole world nowadays does a man throw stones or bow down in that place or do any of these things for idolatrous reasons, neither in word of mouth nor in intention, but his heart is only for God.

As for the way your teacher treated you, calling you a fool and putting you to shame and upsetting you, he has committed a great sin and is guilty of a great transgression. But it seems to me that he did it unintentionally. It would be right for him to beg you to forgive him, even though you are his pupil, and he should then fast, and cry to God and humble himself, and perhaps God will forgive him and allow him to atone for his sin. Was he drunk that he did not realize that in no less than thirty-six places the Torah warns us to behave well toward the convert to Judaism! And what of the verse: "Thou shalt not wrong a stranger" (Exodus 22:20), which refers to wronging with words! Even if he were in the right and you were wrong he would still have been obliged to speak gently to you, how much more so when you are right and he in error!

Furthermore, this man was concerned with whether the Arabs are idolators or not. He should have considered what his own status is once he has flown into a temper, to be angry, unlawfully, with a righteous convert to Judaism. Our Rabbis say that if anyone flies into a rage it should be in your eyes as if he had worshipped idols!

You should know how great is our obligation toward strangers who are converted to Judaism. We are commanded to honor and respect our parents and we are commanded to obey the prophets. It is possible for a man to respect and to honor and to obey someone for whom he has no love. But with regard to strangers we are commanded to love them with a great love coming from the heart just as we are commanded to love God. God Himself in all His glory loves the stranger, as it is said: "He loves the stranger, providing him with food and clothing" (Deuteronomy 10:18).

As for his calling you a fool, I am utterly astonished. A man capable of leaving his father and his birthplace and the protection afforded by the government of his people; a man capable of so much understanding as to attach himself to a people, which today is despised by others and is a slave to rulers, because he appreciates that theirs is the true religion; a man capable of so understanding the ways of Israel as to recognize that all the other religions have stolen from this one, one adding, the other subtracting, one changing, the other lying and attributing to God things that are not so, one destroying foundations, the other speaking topsy-turvy things; a man capable of recognizing all this, pursuing after God, passing through the way of holiness, entering under the wings of the Divine Presence, casting himself at the dust of the feet of Moses our teacher, head of all the prophets, on whom be peace, and desiring God's laws; a man whose heart has led him to come near to the light of life, to ascend the degrees of the angels, and to rejoice and take delight in the joys of the righteous; a man capable of casting this world from his heart, not turning to lies and falsehood; shall such a man be called a fool? God forbid! No fool has God called you but wise, understanding, upright, a pupil of our father Abraham who left his father and his birthplace to go after God.

He who blessed Abraham your teacher, giving him his reward both in this world and the next, may He bless you and give you fitting reward in this world and the next and may He prolong your days until you teach the laws of God to all His congregation and may He give you the merit of witnessing all the consolations destined for Israel. That goodness which God has spoken for us will be yours, too, for the Lord has spoken good for Israel.

> Moses son of Maimon
> the memory of the righteous
> is for a blessing.

Obadiah, the person to whom Maimonides' reply is addressed, was a convert to Judaism from Islam. He was evidently a scholar and Maimonides in the letter looks forward to him being a teacher of the Torah. When the letter was written, however, he had a teacher who, it appears, insulted him when he dared to argue that Muslims are not idolators. The question was more than an academic one. The Talmud lays down certain rules about a Jew's dealing with idolators and it was very important to know whether these applied to Jews who lived, as so many of them did in Maimonides' day, in Islamic lands. For instance, it is forbidden for a Jew to do any business with an idolator three days before any of the idolator's festivals, and it is forbidden for a Jew to have any benefit from wine handled by an idolator. Would these laws apply to Muslims? Maimonides, like many teachers in the Middle Ages, argued that by no stretch of the imagination can Muslims be treated as if they were idolators since they worship the one God and no other.

In Talmudic times an illustration of idolatrous worship that is frequently quoted is that of "throwing stones to Mercury." Mercury was the god of travelers and it appeared that shrines to Mercury were set up by the wayside to which passers-by would pay homage by throwing a stone. It is clear that in Arab lands the Roman god was not worshipped but there was, apparently, an ancient custom to throw stones at the Kaaba at Mecca. The teacher of Obadiah argued that this and similar customs are idolatrous and hence the Muslims are idolators. When Obadiah, who, as a convert from Islam, knew that this was false, remonstrated with his teacher, the latter called him a fool. The poor convert turned to Maimonides, as a great Jewish thinker and teacher, to find out if he was right. Maimonides sided entirely with Obadiah. His reply discusses two questions. The first is the point at issue—whether the Muslims are idolators. The second is the way in which converts to Judaism should be treated.

Maimonides first states that it is necessary to be fair to the Muslims and since, in fact, they are not idolators they should not be said to be such. It appears that some Muslims in Maimonides' day, perhaps through confusing Judaism with Christianity, said that the Jews believed that God has a son. That is to say, the Muslims falsely claimed that the Jews were not pure monotheists. Two wrongs do not make a right, says Maimonides. If they express false opinions about our faith that is no reason for us to express false opinions about theirs. Maimonides does not, of course, believe in any way in the truth of Islam. (The term used in this letter for their "place of worship" is "their place of shame.") But he believes that one must not seek to defend the truth with false arguments and no service is done to Judaism by saying that Muslims are idolators when, in fact, they are nothing of the kind.

Maimonides acknowledges that the Arabs were idolators before the rise of Islam, but, he says, the Arabs themselves will be the first to admit this. The fact that they use the old place of worship and retain certain customs which had their origin in idolatrous practices does not make them into idolators because their heart is now purely for God in their worship. The reference to the "wicked Jews" is to the informers, Jews who were only too ready to inform against their fellow-Jews in order to curry favor with the Arab authorities. Maimonides says here that he could explain at length why he thinks Islam too contains elements of folly but he is afraid to write this down because the letter may fall into the hands of Jewish informers. But, for all its errors, Islam is not an idolatrous faith.

Actually some of the details Maimonides then gives of the three gods are taken from the Talmud and they hardly referred to the ancient gods of the Arabian desert. Peor, for example, was the Baal referred to in the Book of Numbers. However, the main point Maimonides wishes to make is that granted the Muslims still carry out practices which had their origin in idolatrous rites, origins do not really matter, since the intention of present-day Muslims is to worship God and God alone.

The rest of the reply explains itself. Maimonides' father was no longer alive when this letter was written, hence Maimonides signs himself "the son of Maimon the memory of the righteous is for a blessing."

Are grandchildren the legal equivalent of children?

The interpretation of a contract in which the term "grandchildren" occurs.

The following is a Responsum of Ritba, ed. Kapah, Jerusalem, 1959, No. 134. *The Ritba is Rabbi Yom Tov Ben Avraham Ishbili, the famous Spanish Talmudist of the fourteenth century.*

QUESTION: **The community drew up rules for the purposes of communal taxation. In one paragraph of the book of rules it was stated that if a man or woman belonging to the community married off a daughter or a sister to someone who does not pay taxes then there is a tax on the dowry. Now Reuven, who has a daughter, married off his granddaughter to a man who does not pay taxes. The community demands of Reuven that he should pay tax on the dowry in obedience to the above-mentioned paragraph. Reuven's contention is that the paragraph in question refers to a daughter or a sister and he married off neither a daughter nor a sister. That which he has given to his granddaughter is as if it were given to a stranger and for such a gift there is no taxation. The community retorted that grandchildren are always treated in Jewish law as children and the Rabbis say that a man calls his son's son: "My son." Since, then, the girl Reuven** has married off is his granddaughter it is as if he had married off his daughter. Reuven retorted that in spite of all this grandchildren are not like children. The expression used by the Rabbis shows the correctness of this. For the Rabbis say that grandchildren are *like* children, that is to say in the love one bears them, and a man calls a grandson a son because of the love he bears him and because he is so fond of him. But with regard to other matters the term "children" does not include grandchildren. If, for example, a man gave his property to his sons without specifying further, it is obvious that the grandchildren would not have a share in the property. But the community pleads further that there is a clause in the book of rules which states that where there is any doubt as to how the rules are to be interpreted, the interpretation of the communal officers is to be accepted as binding and the communal officers have decided in this case to interpret the laws so that Reuven's granddaughter is treated as his daughter. But Reuven objects that the right of interpretation only applies where the language is obscure. But here it is as clear as anything can be that the term "daughter" does not mean a granddaughter.

REPLY: With all due respect I must agree with Reuven. The reason is that although the Rabbis say that grandchildren are like children as it is stated in tractate *Yevamot (62b)* and they derive it from Scriptural verses, they only say this with regard to Scriptural verses and with regard to the duty of having children, in which case the purpose is for the world to be inhabited and this happens even if there are grandchildren. But as language is used by men in their dealings with one another the term "children" does not include grandchildren. This can be seen from the ruling in tractate *Bava Batra (143b)* in which the following is said: "A certain man before he died said he wished his property to be given to his children and he had a son and a grandson. The question is whether a man refers to his grandson as his son. Mar, son of Rav Ashi, said: "A man never calls his grandson his son." Now the Talmud goes on to say there that we have been taught in an earlier source a teaching in support of Mar, son of Rav Ashi. For it has been taught that if a man takes a vow that he will have no benefit from his sons, he is permitted to have benefit from his grandsons. And we follow the ruling of Mar, son of Rav Ashi, since the earlier source agrees with him.

It follows that according to the law, people do not call their grandchildren children. As the Talmud says: The language of Scripture is one thing, the language of people, in their dealings with one another, is another thing. It is clear from numerous passages in the Talmud that with regard to gifts and vows and so, too, with regard to all agreements between men, whether between individuals or in communal life, we follow the sense as understood in the language of men, whether the law is strict or lenient as a result.

It follows, too, that when Reuven claims the communal officers have no right to decide what the rules mean in this case, he has right on his side. For this is not a matter of doubt but of certainty. With regard to vows, for instance, where the offense is Biblical, we say that one who vows will have no benefit from his sons yet may have benefit from his grandsons. This shows clearly that it is not a matter of doubt, for if it were we know that in matters of Biblical law we always take the stricter view where there is a doubt. It is certain, therefore, that the law is as we have said.

In the Middle Ages the Jewish community was a kind of little state within a larger state and was responsible for operating all of its various communal services. Jewish communities had the right of imposing taxes of various kinds on their members. So the question now explains itself. Ritba sides with Reuven because whatever Scripture might say this is not the way people normally use language in their dealings with one another. In practical law we are not concerned to discover the meaning Scripture puts on the term historically speaking but what those who drew up the rules of the community meant by the term. The reference to the world being inhabited is as follows. The ruling is given in the Talmud that if a man's children had died but he had grandchildren, he has carried out the religious duty of having children. But Ritba says that only here are grandchildren treated as children because it is a religious duty to have children to keep God's world inhabited and this is fulfilled with whatever offspring a man has.

Ritba finally faces the possibility that it might be argued that where the language of people differs in this matter from the language of Scripture it is not certain that we follow the usage of people but we only follow it because this may be the law. In other words, where there is doubt in interpretation the laws give the communal officers the right to put their interpretation on the law. Ritba therefore shows that we follow the language of people not out of doubt but because this is the certain law. His proof is from the ruling that the language of people is followed in connection with vows. Now the general principle is that wherever there is a doubt in matters of Biblical (as opposed to Rabbinic) law the stricter view is always to be taken. Therefore if it were a question of doubt the stricter view would have been taken and since, in fact, it is not, this shows quite conclusively that the language of people is followed not out of doubt but of certainty.

CHAPTER 29

A question of luck

*The laws governing the luck of the
draw in a raffle.*

*Rabbi Jair Ḥayyim Bacharach was born in 1639 and died in 1702. He
was one of the most prominent German Rabbis of his day. Rabbis
addressed many questions to him and these together with his replies
he published under the title: Ḥavvot Jair, "Jair's Encampments," see
Deuteronomy chapter 3, verse 14. There is also a clever pun here
since Ḥavvah is the Hebrew for Eve. The author's grandmother Eve
Bacharach was a learned Jewish woman and he called the work
after her.*

I have a group of householders who study with me and follow my
decisions in Jewish law. One Purim, after they had feasted well and
their hearts were glad with wine, twelve of them decided to raffle a
large silver cup, each one of them giving a Reichstaler. This is
how the raffle is organized. They bring two boxes or two dishes. Into
one of these they place twelve cards, each with one of their names.
Into the other they place another twelve cards, eleven of them blank
and one with the words *Mazzal Tov* inscribed. A little boy or girl then
takes a card at a time from each box and the name which comes out
together with the *Mazzal Tov* card wins. Now it happened in our case

that the *Mazzal Tov* card came out at the second dip and everyone was surprised at the *Mazzal Tov* card emerging so quickly. One of them then examined the cards and discovered that instead of eleven blank cards there were only ten and that *Mazzal Tov* had been written on two of the cards. Now the winner argued that however the mistake was made, whether intentionally or unintentionally or as a joke, none of the contestants had, in fact, any more advantage or disadvantage than his fellows. Consequently, if luck was with him now it would have been so even if the affair had been managed properly.

I ruled that it is obvious that the raffle is null and void for we follow the ruling of Rav who rules, in the case of the brother who came from a distant land, that the division is cancelled. This in the Chapter *Bet Kor* page 106b and is to be found in the *Tur Ḥoshen Mishpat*, and in the *Shulḥan Arukh,* chapter 175.

They raffled the cup a second time and this time one of them won at the sixth draw. One of the men whose name remained on an undrawn card happened to take a look at the remaining name cards and he discovered that one of the names had been left out and that only eleven name cards had been placed in the box. Now the members of the group wished this draw, too, to be cancelled but the winner insisted that there was no reason to cancel the draw because one name had been omitted. On the contrary, he argued, since a name was missing the others had a better chance of winning. As for the man whose name had been left out, the winner was prepared to compensate him by giving him four Reichstalers and he was quite willing to accept this. Now at first glance the decision seemed right to me without more ado. But after further reflection, from the sea to the frying pan, I decided that here, too, the raffle is null and void.

My argument was that we see, in the case of the brother who came from a distant land, that even if they had three fields of equal value, and each brother took a field and a half, each of them can have the division cancelled when the third brother turns up. This would apply even when the brothers wrote out three cards each with the name of a field, and the third brother picked out the field which they had previously divided and was quite satisfied with the draw. Nevertheless each one of the first two can claim to have the original division cancelled completely. These are the words of Ri in the *Tosaphot* there and so it is ruled in the *Shulḥan Arukh* there. Even though, rationally speaking, there is no reason or cause for either of them to protest, nevertheless a lottery which has been improperly conducted has no validity, how much more so when the fault is in the lottery itself!

For we see that in the Torah, in the Prophets and in the Hagiographa they relied on a lottery when it was done without any human interference or human skill. The land was divided by lot. And they relied on the lot to kill Achan and Jonathan, too, were it not that here the people redeemed him, and he was saved by his confession. And it is said: "The lot is cast into the lap; but the whole disposing thereof is of the Lord" (Proverbs 16:33). And even among the nations of the world this seems to have been accepted as in the case of Jonah and the wicked Haman according to the plain sense of Scripture. For it is probable that where the lottery is carried out correctly God's Providence attaches itself to it, as it is said: "Declare the right" (I Samuel 14:41). It is otherwise where the lottery has been interfered with, then there is no cause for saying that it is from God. Whether the interference was by trickery or by accident the lottery has been done and each one of the contestants can argue: If the lottery had been properly conducted my luck would have held or my prayer that I may be successful in all my dealings would have been answered. This can be seen from the argument in *Bava Metzia* page 106a that the lessor can say to the lessee: "The verse would have been fulfilled for me"; "Thou shalt also decree a thing and it shall be established for thee" (Job 22:28). And as it is said: "Thou maintainest my lot" (Psalms 16:5). Even though it appears from the *Tosaphists* at the bottom of the page that this does not apply to a general prayer, for all that a lottery is in a different category since it is in any event a means of assuring the help of Providence if it is carried out properly.

It seems to me that even more than all this is true. If a man fraudulently slipped two cards with his name upon them into the box and another person drew the winning card and when the trickster admitted it they investigated and found as he had said, the others can have the raffle declared null and void and even the trickster himself can have it so declared. I have written as it seemed right to my humble mind.

Jair Ḥayyim Bacharach

It appears that while heavy gambling cannot have been approved of by the Rabbis they did not object, in Rabbi Bacharach's day, to an occasional flutter. In those days householders would deem it their duty to gather around a learned Rabbi each evening for the purpose of Torah study. On the feast of Purim it would naturally tend to celebrate as a group. The prize in the particular raffle with which we are concerned was an expensive silver cup. Each of the contestants put into the "kitty" a German dollar (a Reichstaler) to pay for the cup and the winner would keep the cup. Mazzal Tov means "Good luck." Rabbi Bacharach says that the players were surprised that the winning card was drawn so quickly because the chances are against it being drawn immediately.

The winner rested his case on the fact that he had no greater advantage and no greater chance of winning than any of the other players, even though there were, in fact, two winning cards. He had had the good fortune to win and he should be allowed to keep the prize.

Brilliantly Rabbi Bacharach quotes from a Talmudic discussion to show that the winner's claim should be rejected and that the raffle was null and void. The passage to which he refers is called "Bet Kor" and is in Tractate Bava Batra of the Babylonian Talmud page 106b. The case there is as follows. A father died leaving his two sons three fields. The sons, wishing to divide up the estate, cast lots to determine which part of the estate should belong to either. After each brother had received his field and a half by the casting of lots a third brother, hitherto unknown, turned up and established by law his right to a share in the estate. Samuel, the great Babylonian teacher of the third century, rules that they can each hold on to the field which has fallen to them but they each must give half a field to the third brother. Rav, however, argues that since the lottery was inaccurate (for there should have been three brothers involved, not two) the whole affair is null and void and they must all three ballot again. Rav's ruling is followed in the two Codes of Jewish law, the Tur and the Shulḥan Arukh. Consequently, says Rabbi Bacharach, in our case, too, the raffle is null and void.

The group evidently decided to accept the Rabbi's ruling and they tried again with a further mishap (remember it was Purim and there had been a good deal of heavy drinking). This time only eleven names, instead of twelve, had been placed in the box. Obviously the man whose name had been omitted has a case, but this is not at issue here since the winner was prepared to compensate him and he was willing to accept. But the losers naturally wished to invalidate the draw. The winner claimed that the omission of a name had merely served to increase the chances of the other eleven but had in no way affected the luck of the draw. At first Rabbi Bacharach was inclined to agree with this. This was different from the first case where the winning card might not have come up so soon if there were only one!

But on reflection (from the sea to the frying pan i.e. the time it takes to catch a fish, a Talmudic expression) the Rabbi decided against the winner. His argument is based on the Talmudic passage already quoted. Rav's ruling would be applied even when the two brothers took one field each by lot and simply divided up the third field and even where the third brother drew the third field. This is exactly the same as our case for here, too, the luck of the draw was not affected by the appearance of the third brother. Rabbi Bacharach quotes in his support one of the Tosaphists who gives this explanation. The Tosaphists are French commentators to the Talmud in the twelfth and thirteenth centuries, whose notes are printed in most editions of the Talmud. One of the most prominent of the Tosaphists was Rabbi Isaac son of Samuel of Dampierre, mentioned here, and called after the initials of his name Ri (Rabbi Isaac). Rabbi Bacharach agrees that the luck of the draw is not directly affected but he introduces a rather curious argument. This is that the draw can be said to have divine control, provided it is left entirely to chance. But where there is human interference of any kind the divine guidance cannot, as it were, operate.

He tries to prove his contention by citing the references to casting lots and so forth in the Torah (the Five Books of Moses), the Prophets and the Hagiographa (the Sacred Writings e.g. Psalms, Esther and so forth). He quotes a number of examples of how Scripture relies on the lot to determine certain events.

First he quotes the reliance on the lot for dividing up the land promised to the children of Israel (see Numbers 26:52-56). It is rather surprising that he does not refer to Leviticus 16:7-9. The story of Achan is in the book of Joshua, chapter 7, the story of Jonathan in First Samuel, chapter 14. For the lots cast for Jonah see the book of Jonah and for the story of Haman see Esther 3:7. Notice the rather cautious way in which Rabbi Bacharach says that God's Providence attaches itself to it.

A further quote is now given. Rabbi Bacharach argues that the losers can claim that for all we know to the contrary if the raffle had not been interfered with their prayers would have been answered i.e. someone else might have won. That this is so, he says, can be seen from the discussion in Tractate Bava Metzia of the Babylonian Talmud page 106a. (It is merely a coincidence that both Talmudic passages quoted are on page 106 of different Tractates but a coincidence of this kind is perhaps not unsuitable in a discussion of chance.)

The case in Bava Metzia is as follows. A lessee is a man who rents a field from another (the lessor) not for money but on the understanding that he will work the field and give the lessor a share in the profits. The lessor can make any conditions he chooses. Suppose, then, he orders the lessee to sow wheat in the field but the lessee disregards his orders and sows barley. The whole area is smitten with drought and the crop fails. Has the lessee to compensate the lessor for his loss because he has disobeyed his orders? The lessee argues that since the loss was by natural causes, not through his negligence, he has no obligation to compensate the lessor. But the lessor argues, and his argument is accepted in the Talmudic passage, that the lessee cannot say that even if he had obeyed orders and sown wheat the crop would have failed. For the lessor may have prayed for a good wheat crop and the prayer may have been effective were it not for the fact that barley had been sown. God, in the words of the Rabbis, fulfills the decree (the prayer) of the righteous. Similarly, says Rabbi Bacharach, the losers can say that otherwise their prayer might have helped.

The Rabbi remarks further that he is well aware that the Tosaphists in their comment at the foot of this page argue that the case is different when the lessor gives the lessee the right to sow whatever he chooses. Here he cannot argue that it is the lessee's bad luck and that otherwise his prayer would have helped. For to expect a "general" prayer (i.e. not a prayer for something particular like a wheat crop) to be effective is to expect a miracle and miracles do not happen so readily. Now in our case the losers claim that their general prayers for success might have been effective and this is contradicted by the Tosaphists. To this the reply is given that success by a lottery is in a different category because, as stated before, there is an element of divine guidance in a lottery if properly conducted.

CHAPTER 30

NODA BI-YEHUDAH, SECTION ON ORAḤ ḤAYYIM

Innovations in Synagogue architecture

The laws governing the building of a Synagogue
in an unusual shape.

The following is a Responsum of Rabbi Ezekiel Landau, Noda
Bi-Yehudah, *"Known in Judah,"* Tinyana, *"Second Collection,"*
Stettin, 1861, *section on* Oraḥ Ḥayyim, *"The Way of Life,"* No. 18,
pages 9a–b. Rabbi Landau was Rabbi of Prague, where he died in
1793. His Responsa are among the most famous of all time.

To Triest.   The 12th day of Tishri, 5548

Written before the Sukkot festival to his honor, my friend, whom my
soul loves, the famous scholar and leader Rabbi Asher, may God
protect him.

I have received your letter. With regard to the question whether
it is permitted to build a Synagogue with eight walls and eight corners or whether a Synagogue must have only four walls and four
corners and must be greater in length than in breadth, I am surprised
at the questioner. What reason can he have had for supposing that
it is forbidden? You were quite right to tell him that there is no reference to this in the *Shulḥan Arukh*. I go further and say that we do
not find in any of the early Codes or in the Babylonian Talmud or
the Jerusalem Talmud that a Synagogue is required to have any par-

ticular shape. To be on the safe side I shall prove to you that it is permitted.

I quote the words of the Rashba in Responsum No. 585. "Reuven had a house adjoining the Ark of a Synagogue. The house was beautifully built and he wished to donate it to the Synagogue so that it should form part of a larger Synagogue. But the congregation protested that the result would be that the seats of the Synagogue would be reduced in value . . ." Read that Responsum carefully.

Now it is obvious that Reuven's house was not equal in width to the east wall of the Synagogue in which the Ark was fixed. For if this were so it would have been necessary, when Reuven donated his house, to demolish the whole eastern wall of the Synagogue in order to increase the size of the Synagogue. The eastern wall of Reuven's house would then have become the new eastern wall of the Synagogue and the Ark which was formerly in the eastern wall of the Synagogue would now be in the eastern wall of Reuven's house, which would now be the new eastern wall of the Synagogue. But in that case how would the value of the seats be affected? All the seats that were previously fixed to the right and left of the Ark in the eastern part of the Synagogue could again be fixed in the new eastern part to the right and left of the Ark. Each seat would be as near to the Ark as it was previously. And so, too, the seats in the north and south near to the east would now, too, be in the north and south of the new eastern wall, each in turn near to the east. They would have exactly the same value as before. All that would happen would be that to the north and south at the western end of the Synagogue there would be room for more seats. It is forced to suggest that the protest of the congregation was on the grounds that by increasing the number of seats in the Synagogue the value of all the seats would go down, because there would be a greater supply of seats, for this is not implied in the language of the Responsum. The words "the seats be reduced in value" suggest that the concern is with the loss of value of the seats in themselves not because the price will go down.

It is also forced to suggest that the *Bimah* was fixed in the center of the Synagogue so that now if the eastern seats will be fixed in the eastern wall of Reuven's house they will be farther from the *Bimah* than they were and their occupants will not be able to hear as well as before. For this, too, is not suggested by the words "the seats be reduced in value."

It is also forced to suggest that the seats around the *Bimah* would be farther from the Ark than they were, for this, too, would not fall under the heading of loss of value since in any event there would be nothing in the way between these seats and the Ark and no new seats would have been fixed between them and the Ark.

Apart from this, the words of the Responsum: "adjoining the Ark of a Synagogue" do not suggest that the width of Reuven's house was equal to that of the Synagogue wall for if that were the case we should have expected the words to be: "adjoining the Ark wall of the Synagogue."

Consequently, it appears that the width of Reuven's house was less than the width of the Synagogue wall and was only as wide as the Ark and a little more at either side but did not reach as far as the ends of the Synagogue to the north and south. If they had widened the limits of the Synagogue they would have done this by removing the Ark from its place and breaking through the wall into the space occupied by Reuven's house. The Synagogue space would then have been greater in the middle but exactly the same on either side to the north and the south so that the new east wall in Reuven's house would have been incapable of taking all the former seats which were in the eastern wall of the Synagogue. These seats would have remained on either side of the east wall but they would now have been more distant from the Ark and would lose their value.

Now it is clear that if it were not for the question of loss of value Reuven would have been permitted to add his house to the Synagogue. But in that case the Synagogue would have had seven walls and six corners! Therefore the words of the one who would forbid it have no validity.

All this I said in accordance with the strict letter of the law. But I wonder why they should want to do this and I thought that perhaps they saw something like this in the palaces of princes or in some other houses and they wanted to copy it. But the truth is that it is not proper for us in our exile to copy princes and to be envious of them. If this was the reason, I recite for this the verse: "And Israel hath forgotten his Maker, and builded palaces" (Hosea 8:14). It is better, therefore, not to change any of the old customs, especially in this generation. But if their reason was that there would be more room if the Synagogue is built according to these specifications there is not the slightest fear of anything wrong. I have to cut this discussion short because I am very busy.

The Responsum is addressed to a scholar in Triest who had consulted Rabbi Landau. The 12th day of Tishri is, of course, between Yom Kippur and Sukkot. The year 5548 corresponds to the year 1787. Note the flowery titles which belonged to the fashion of those days. We know that the old Synagogue in Triest was destroyed by fire and that a magnificent new Synagogue was erected in 1787! See the article on "Triest" in the Jewish Encyclopedia, Vol. XII, page 259.

The question is whether it is permitted to depart from the usual custom of building a Synagogue with four walls (an oblong) to build an octagonal Synagogue. Most Synagogues were oblong and followed a more or less standard pattern. No doubt in Triest at that time it was decided to experiment with a new design and some scholar had questioned the propriety of this. Rabbi Asher had replied that he saw no objection to the new style but in order to make sure he evidently addressed a question on the subject to Rabbi Landau as the outstanding authority in Jewish law. Rabbi Landau follows the old rule that if there is no reason for prohibiting any innovations they are automatically permitted. No reason is required for permission if there can be produced no reason for prohibiting. The Shulḥan Arukh, the standard Code of Jewish Law, makes no reference to any prohibition and, says Rabbi Landau, there are no ancient rules in any of the sources regarding the shape of a Synagogue. We are therefore safe in concluding that Synagogue architecture can be left to the discretion of the architect. But, not content with this conclusion, Rabbi Landau goes on to prove that it is permitted.

The Rashba is Rabbi Solomon Ben Abraham Adret (1235-1310) known as "The Rabbi of Spain" i.e. the foremost authority on Jewish law in Spain during his period. His works still enjoy great authority so that it was natural for Rabbi Landau to base his decision on Rashba's opinion. Note how skillfully Rabbi Landau quotes the particular Responsum of Rashba which has nothing to do with his question but from which it can be inferred by the clever analysis to which he subjects Rashba's words.

Rashba's question has to do with a certain person (designated Reuven, the usual symbol in this literature for "a certain person" much as we would say "A"), who owned a fine house adjoining the Ark of a Synagogue and who wished to give the house as a gift so that the Synagogue could be enlarged. The effect of this, however, would be to change the order of seating and the change would have the effect of devaluating the seats. Hence it can be argued that the congregation have every right to refuse the gift because they prefer a smaller Synagogue with more valuable seats to a large one in which their seats have lost some of their value. Rabbi Landau proceeds to show that if we examine Rashba's case carefully we shall see that the proposed alteration would result in a Synagogue with more than four walls and four corners. And yet Rashba is only concerned with the question of congregational rights. But if a Synagogue must have four walls and four corners Rashba should have ruled, on grounds of religious law, that Reuven's suggestion cannot be accepted. This is a conclusive proof that there is no law that a Synagogue must be oblong and Rashba's opinion in such a matter can be taken as final.

Rabbi Landau first proves that in Rashba's case the conditions were not such that all that would have been required, if Reuven's gift had been accepted, was for the dividing wall between the house and the Synagogue to be removed, the house being the same width as the Synagogue. If this were the case the new Synagogue would be no different in shape from the old. All that Reuven's gift would have done would have been to have added to the area of the Synagogue. If this is Rashba's case it is hard to see what the congregation was objecting to. All the seats could simply have been moved forward, nearer to the Ark in the newest wall (i.e. the eastern wall of what was formerly Reuven's house). (The seats in Synagogues were generally placed in a square around the Bimah, the reading desk, in the center of the Synagogue. Some of the seats were on either side of the Ark. These were the best seats. The others were placed facing inwards at the north and south sides of the Synagogues.) When all the seats had been moved forward none of the older congregants would be any the worse. But there would now be room for more seats at the far end of the Synagogue for the use of new congregants.

It might be argued, says Rabbi Landau, that this was, indeed, so and the protest of the congregation is precisely on these grounds that the more seats there are in the Synagogue the cheaper they all become because there is less competition for seats. But Rabbi Landau thinks it far-fetched to interpret Rashba in this way. His concern seems to be that the positioning of the seats in the new building affects their value, not the fact that there are more seats.

Similarly, Rabbi Landau considers it forced to suggest that the positioning in question has to do with the greater distance from the Ark or the Bimah. In any event, he goes on to say, if the size of Reuven's house were exactly the same as the size of the Ark wall in width Rashba would have formulated the question differently. Instead of saying that the house adjoined the Ark he would have said the house adjoined the Ark wall. In any legal document or ruling the wording of the lawyers is always very precise and Rashba as a great lawyer would have been very careful to express himself accurately.

We are left with the conclusion that, in fact, in Rashba's case the addition would have been only in the middle of the Ark wall. The new building would then be an oblong with a further oblong or recess in the middle of the eastern wall. This would be a case of a seven-walled, six-cornered Synagogue. And yet Rashba only objects on the grounds of the congregation's protest. But if the congregation accepted willingly Reuven's gift there would be no cause for any objection, which demonstrates that there can be no objection to having a Synagogue with more than four walls and four corners.

Rabbi Landau sees fit, however, to add a few words. Some things may well be permitted if all we go on is the strict letter of the law, but they may offend the spirit of Jewish law. Motives are here important. Rabbi Landau is a bit dubious about the motives of those who wish to depart from the normal architectural style. If their motive was simply to "show off" by copying other splendid buildings they had seen, such ostentation is not really befitting to a people in exile. The Jews in Europe at the end of the eighteenth century were not too badly off but they suffered much from discrimination and Rabbi Landau feels that they should not try to "poke out the eyes" of their neighbors in building showy structures for worship. They would then rather be worshipping themselves instead of God. Hence his quotation from Hosea.

Rabbi Landau's reference to "this generation" probably has to be understood as a protest against the new winds of change that were then blowing in the Jewish world which many Rabbis at the time felt may lead to a rejection of ancient Jewish laws. But if their motives were simply in order to have more room, what objection could there be? In other words if the new style were wrong in itself it would be wrong even if the motives were worthy. But Rabbi Landau has proved that the style is not wrong in itself and can only be faulted if the motive is unworthy. It follows that if the motives are worthy there can be no objection.

CHAPTER 31

RESPONSA OF RABBI DAVID HOFFMANN, MELAMMED LE-HOIL, VOL. II,
FRANKFORT, 1926, NO. 104, PAGES 108–9

A dangerous but necessary operation

*The law governing the right of a parent to object
to an operation on his child.*

*Rabbi David Hoffmann was one of the foremost Rabbis and teachers
in Germany at the beginning of this century. He taught at the
famous Rabbinical Seminary in Berlin for nearly fifty years, becoming
President of the Institution in 1902. Questions were addressed
to him by many Rabbis and the following is one of his replies.*

QUESTION: **If the parents of a sick child refuse to give permission
to the surgeon to perform an operation on the child, is he obliged
nonetheless to perform it? The question can be sub-divided as
follows: a) Where the surgeon believes that the operation will be
successful; b) Where the surgeon is doubtful whether the operation
will be successful but where it is clear that unless the operation is
performed the child will certainly die.**

REPLY: **Behold the essential problem here is whether the possibility
of saving the child permanently is sufficient to push aside the
possibility that his temporal existence may be cut short. Now the
case has been decided in the Responsa collection:** *Shevut Yaakov*

Part III, No. 75, regarding a certain sick person of whom the doctors diagnosed that he would undoubtedly die within one or two days. But, they said, there is a possible means of healing him but it is also possible that if this means is resorted to and is unsuccessful he will die immediately. The author rules that it is permitted to have resort to the doubtful cure. Even though it is obvious that it is forbidden to shorten life and whoever shortens life even for a moment is a murderer, nevertheless where it is possible that the sick person will be completely cured by this means one need not take into account the possibility that as a result his life may be shortened. He produced a number of conclusive arguments for his decision, especially from the Talmudic passage, *Avodah Zarah* page 27b. His conclusion is that nonetheless the doctor should not act on his own accord but should consult the other expert doctors of the town and they should act in accordance with the majority opinion. By a majority in this connection is meant a clear majority i.e. a two-thirds majority. Since, then, it is permitted to perform the operation in these circumstances it certainly follows that the opinion of the parents has no effect one way or the other. For it is ruled in *Yoreh Deah* chapter 336 that a doctor has an obligation to heal and if he refuses he is guilty of shedding blood. We do not find anywhere in the Torah that parents have a right to endanger the lives of their children by preventing the doctor from performing his craft. This is the law of the Torah, but what the law of the land has to say in this case I do not know.

We have here an actual case that was submitted to Rabbi Hoffmann. Basically the question concerns the correct attitude for the doctor to adopt in such a case if he wishes to act in accordance with Jewish law. It is a matter of Jewish medical ethics. But in the particular case the subject is further complicated because evidently the parents had refused in any circumstances to allow the operation to be performed. Rabbi Hoffmann essentially takes the line that the parents have no say in the matter and that if the doctor is permitted to perform the operation, in accordance with Jewish law, then he must go ahead and perform it in spite of the parents' objection. If, on the other hand, Jewish law does not permit it, then the parents have no right to demand it. What we have to consider therefore is whether Jewish law permits it. Now if the doctor believes that the operation will be successful it must be carried out even though, as in every operation, there is an element of risk. If this were not so we would have to conclude that Jewish law forbids any operations, which is obviously not so. If, on the other hand, the operation is known to be an especially risky one and there is the danger that it may kill the patient, it would not normally be permitted. In our case, however, the patient will die in any event so what one has to balance is the risk of him dying now. Which is better, that he should be allowed to survive for a few days and then die for sure or that the doctor should try to save his life for good by taking the risk of killing him under the knife?

Sometimes the Rabbi to whom such a question is addressed has no precedents to guide him in his decision, but here Rabbi Hoffmann finds that the very same question has been addressed to Rabbi Jacob Reischer (died 1733) and his reply was published in his Responsa collection under the title: Shevut Yaakov. The science of anatomy had not, of course, been developed in Rabbi Reischer's day so that his question does not concern an operation, but the principle is the same. Normally, argues Rabbi Reischer, it is as much an act of murder in Jewish law to shorten life as to take it (if, for instance, someone kills an incurable he is still guilty of murder because he takes away from him the short time he has to live). But in our case the risk is worth taking because the result might be that the patient is completely cured.

Rabbi Reischer proves his case from the passage in the Babylonian Talmud, Tractate Avodah Zarah page 27b. In those days there was a peculiar law (but one which becomes intelligible if we consider the background of the time when many heathen considered it to be no wrong to kill a Jew), that a Jew must not allow himself to be treated by a heathen physician who might kill him. In those circumstances to have recourse to a heathen physician was to risk one's life, which was forbidden. But, says the Talmud, supposing the Jew knows that if he does not have resort to the heathen physician he will certainly die in a few days time whereas, although he takes the risk of immediate death, if he places himself in the physician's hand he may be cured. What is he to do? The answer is given explicitly that the risk must be taken. A proof is quoted in the Talmud from the verse in II Kings 7:4—"If we say, we will enter the city, then the famine is in the city, and we shall die there: and if we sit still here, we die also. Now, therefore, come and let us fall into the host of the Syrians: if they save us alive, we shall live; and if they kill us, we shall but die."

The story in the book of Kings concerns four lepers who were outside the camp of Israel in a time of famine when the camp was besieged by the Syrians. They argued that to stay where they were or to enter the city was to die of hunger in a day or two whereas to throw themselves on the mercy of the Syrians was to risk immediate death, but it was just possible that the Syrians would save their lives and give them food. The four lepers took the risk and their conduct seems to have been approved by Scripture. From which it follows that it is right to take a risk of immediate death, with the possibility of life being gained, if the alternative is certain loss of life in a short space of time.

Rabbi Reischer is, however, reluctant to allow a single doctor to make decisions of this kind involving life and death and so he rules that a vote be taken of all the doctors available. These should act in accordance with a majority view, not a straight majority but a two-thirds majority i.e. if there were thirty doctors there should be at least twenty for the cure being undertaken.

The Shulḥan Arukh, the standard Code of Jewish Law, in the section Yoreh Deah, clearly places the obligation of healing on the physician. Hence, Rabbi Hoffmann argues, since Rabbi Reischer has argued the case convincingly for the operation to go forward the decision should be that of the doctors, and the parents have no power to hinder the process of healing.

Generally speaking Jewish law takes into account the law of the particular country in which Jews reside. If, for instance, the law of the land was opposed to operations in cases of risk of this kind or if it gave the parents the right to object, the operation would then be illegal according to the law of the land and the Rabbi would not advise the doctors to perform an illegal operation. Hence Rabbi Hoffmann concludes that he stated the position in Jewish law but it would be necessary to determine what the position is in German law.

Glossary

Aggadah: the non-legal part of Rabbinic literature

Aḥaronim: "the later ones," the post-*Shulḥan Arukh* legal authorities

Amora, plural **Amoraim:** the post-Mishnaic teachers in Palestine and Babylon

Baraita, plural **Baraitot:** teachings of the *Tannaim* not included in the Mishnah

bar metzra: "son of the boundary," a man owning a field adjoining another field up for sale has the first option on that field

ben: "son of"

Bet Ha-Midrash: "House of Study," the building attached to or near to the Synagogue in which Torah is studied

Bimah: "Platform" from which the Torah is read in the Synagogue

Gemara: "Teaching," an Aramaic word denoting the discussions of the Palestinian and Babylonian *Amoraim*. The term is synonymous with Talmud. Thus there is a Palestinian Gemara and a Babylonian

genevah: "theft," stealing by stealth

Geonim, singular **Gaon:** "Excellency"; the heads of the Babylonian schools of Sura and Pumbedita from the sixth to the tenth centuries C.E.

gezelah: "robbery," stealing by force directly

geriva: a very small piece of land

Halakhah: from a root meaning "to walk," "the way in which one should walk," the legal side of Judaism, the legal discussions of the Rabbis

Ḥillul Ha-Shem: "Profanation of God's Name"

kav: a small measure of capacity equal to four *log*

Kiddush: literally "sanctification." The prayer welcoming the inception of a Sabbath or festival, customarily recited over a cup of wine

Kiddush Ha-Shem: "Sanctification of God's Name"

kinyan: "acquisition," the formal act to denote that there has been a transfer of property

kor: a large measure of capacity equal to six *kav*

kosher: religiously "fit" or "proper." The term is most closely associated with the dietary laws of Judaism

log: a liquid measure equal to the displacement of six eggs

maneh: one hundred *zuz*

Mappah: "Tablecloth," the notes of Rabbi Moses Isserles to the *Shulḥan Arukh* of Rabbi Joseph Karo

Massekhet: "Web," a Tractate of the Talmud, plural *Massekhtot*

matzah: unleavened bread eaten on Passover

mazzal tov: "good luck"

Mekhilta: "Measure," Rabbinic commentary to the book of Exodus

Midrash, plural **Midrashim:** Rabbinic commentaries to the Bible

Mishnah: "Teaching," the summary of Jewish teaching compiled by Rabbi Judah the Prince at the end of the second century

Mishneh Torah: The title of Maimonides' Code of Jewish Law completed about 1180

perutah: the smallest coin of the realm in Talmudic times

poel: a workman

Rav: the lesser title given to the Babylonian *Amoraim*

Rabbi: the superior title given to the *Tannaim* and the Palestinian *Amoraim*

Rashi: Rabbi Shelomoh ben Yitzḥak, famous French commentator to the Bible and Talmud (1040-1105)

Rishonim: "the early ones," the pre-*Shulḥan Arukh* legal authorities

Seder: "Order," the home service on Passover

sela: a coin worth four *zuz*

She'elot u-Teshuvot: literally, "Questions and Answers," generally used in reference to legal inquiries to and responses of leading Jewish authorities

sheḥitah: the traditional method of killing animals for food

Shema: "Hear," Israel's declaration of faith, Deuteronomy 6:4

Shulḥan Arukh: "Prepared Table," the Code of Rabbi Joseph Karo (1488-1575) with notes (Mappah) by Rabbi Moses Isserles of Cracow (1510-1572)

Siphra: "The Book," the Rabbinic commentary to the book of Leviticus

Siphre: "The Books," the Rabbinic commentary to the books of Numbers and Deuteronomy

Tanna: "Teacher," plural **Tannaim,** the Rabbis of the first two centuries C.E.

terefah: literally "torn," but by extension used of any item which is no longer religiously acceptable. The general usage concerns foods disqualified under the Jewish dietary laws

Torah: "The Law," the Five Books of Moses; Torah also means the sum total of Jewish teaching

Tosaphists: The school of French commentators to the Talmud which flourished in the 12th and 13th centuries

Tosephta: "Supplement," additional source to the Mishnah of *Tannaitic* teachings

Tur: "Row," plural **Turim:** the Code of Jacob ben Asher (14th century), "The Four Rows"

tzaddik: the righteous man

tzedakah: charity, alms-giving

umman: a craftsman

Yad Ha-Ḥazakah: "The Strong Hand," the Code of Maimonides (1135-1204)

Yom Kippur: Day of Atonement

zuz: a copper coin